Boy Soldier

By Clive Thomas

Boy Soldier

Clive Thomas

Published by Clive Thomas

Copyright 2013

Licence Note

All rights reserved. Without limiting the rights under copyright reserved above, no part of this publication may be reproduced, stored in or introduced into a retrieval system, or transmitted in any form, or by any means (electronic, mechanical, photocopying, recording or otherwise) without the prior written permission of both the copyright owner and the above publisher of this book.

This book is licensed for your personal enjoyment only and may not be sold or given away to other people or organisations. If you would like to share this book please purchase another copy for each recipient.

If you are reading this book and did not purchase it, if it was not purchased for your use only, then please return it or purchase your own copy.

Preface

This is a warts and all account of my childhood, some of which is disturbing, some frightening and some plain disgusting. It's the events that lead up to me joining the British Army at 16 as a Junior Driver in the Junior Leaders Regiment of The Royal Corps of Transport a boy soldier.

I tell of the abuse both physical and mental from my parents. The favouritism that my siblings enjoyed, and the resentment my parents had for me. I realised early in my life that what I went through was not normal.

I reveal bullying at school, the friendships I made, and the positive influences like the Husband and Fowler families and teachers like Mr Glan Williams and my athletics coach Andrew Ireland.

Most of all there is hope. There is always a way out, in my case I joined the Army, but I would also like to point out that the abused doesn't have to become an abuser, you have a choice.

Contents

Chapter 1	8
Chapter 2	11
Chapter 3	14
Chapter 4	17
Chapter 5	21
Chapter 6	23
Chapter 7	25
Chapter 8	27
Chapter 9	30
Chapter 10	33
Chapter 11	35
Chapter 12	36
Chapter 13	38
Chapter 14	40
Chapter 15	43
Chapter 16	45
Chapter 17	49
Chapter 18	53
Chapter 19	56
Chapter 20	61
Chapter 21	63
Chapter 22	65
Chapter 23	67
Chapter 24	70
Chapter 25	73
Chapter 26	76
Chapter 27	78

Chapter 28	79
Chapter 29	80
Chapter 30	82
Chapter 31	84
Chapter 32	88
Chapter 33	91
Chapter 34	93
Chapter 35	95
Chapter 36	97
Chapter 37	99
Chapter 38	102
Chapter 39	104
Chapter 40	106
Chapter 41	109
Chapter 42	112
Chapter 43	116
Chapter 44	123
Chapter 45	126
Chapter 46	129
Chapter 47	133
Chapter 48	135
Chapter 49	137
Chapter 50	150
Chapter 51	157
Chapter 52	162
Chapter 53	168
Chapter 54	171
Chapter 55	172
Chapter 56	178
Chapter 57	181
Chapter 58	185
Chapter 59	190

Chapter 60 197
Chapter 61 199
Chapter 62 206
Chapter 63 214

Boy Soldier

Chapter 1

The overriding impression of my childhood is one of unhappiness and loneliness. Nobody really knew how I felt or how I feel now about that time in my life. A song that I can really empathise with is "At The Edge" by Stiff Little Fingers. It starts: "Back when I was young and they were talking AT me, never listened to word I say!"

My earliest recollection was being shipped off to my mother's sister when my sister was born when I was three. Although the memory of this time is quite vague I remember being sent to my aunt's, although my elder brother stayed at home. What the thinking behind this was I have no idea.

I got to know the boys in my neighbourhood when I was about four and starting school. Robert and Simon Fowler lived opposite, Robert was two years older and Simon was a couple of months younger, but because my birthday is in august and Simon's October I was a year above Simon at school. My brother Simon also hung round with us. We hung out played football rugby cricket. Robert immediately took the lead in everything we did. I suppose he made the rules for our little group. I still felt most comfortable in my own company though, it was something I was to get used too until I joined the Army.

I always felt like an outsider from quite an early age, especially within my so called family. My mother always seemed to have it in for me. Punishments far exceeded what ever my siblings received. Although my family's excuse for treating my brother Simon differently was, that Simon was not all there and that he had some sort of brain damage. Simon was always referred to as special. Simon was slower in some aspects, mainly academic. However as Simon got older it was used as an excuse, Simon was not as stupid as he was made out to be, and I am sure he used it to his advantage many times. Simon was always in the lowest academic class. I suppose he was treated as being simple, so I suspect some of that rubbed off. Today I suppose he would be treated as special needs. I was told many times that due to Simon's "condition" it made him completely lose control when he lost his temper. I was also told that because of Simon's "condition" I was not allowed to retaliate in any way shape or form, and that I had to walk away and that I was not even allowed to defend myself. This I believe gave Simon free reign to do what he wanted without any fear of any repercussions.

I know some childhood memories are quite vague I have quite vivid memories of my childhood though. I went to Maendy County Primary School. The head master was a chap called Mr Price-Jones. He was a good headmaster. He ran what he called "The Badge

Club." Mr Price-Jones was a former member of the RAF. Mr Price-Jones has built up a network of military contacts from all over the world. We had visitors from various military personnel from different countries who came to give talks which I found really interesting. Primary school was ok. It was a very small school, with the school split into 3 areas. There was a class room at either side of the school, while the central area was a large room that could be split into two. There were 2 play grounds a separate toilet block and a separate building that was the canteen. I do remember Mrs Norton who was the dinner lady and the school crossing person. Mrs Norton also did play ground duty during the lunch time break. Mrs Norton was a very stern looking woman, and to be honest we were all scared of her.

Chapter 2

I was five the first time my mother told me that she had a baby girl thirteen months before I was born. My mother told me that I was never wanted, she wanted the baby girl that she called "Janey." My mother told me that if "Janey" had survived I would never have been born. This was something that my mother was to say many times. Particularly when I got a bit older and she could no longer to physically intimidate me.

I remember the day in October 1972, when I came home, turned on the radio and listened to the match. It was Llanelli versus New Zealand, which Llanelli won 9 -3. I have supported Llanelli (now the Scarlets) as far back as I could remember. Growing up in Wales, most of the Towns and Cities that have big rugby clubs have English names, such as Cardiff, Newport, Swansea, Bridgend are all English names for Welsh places, where Llanelli was the first place I could pronounce that had a top class rugby team with a Welsh name.

I was never in trouble at school however I was no saint I guess. I tried to fit in. On one particular day, I must have been about six, Robert wanted me to be a look out. Robert and a group of older kids in the top class decided to climb over the school roof. The group were spotted and had fun running round the school then over the roof. I wanted to join in but was told I was too young by the older kids and I was only there to watch out for the teachers. Inevitably they got caught. I was spoken to but as I was only the lookout I wasn't in trouble with the school.

I was always in trouble at home though. Around this time father decided to enforce his table manners on me. Manners he said he was taught at Monkton House Boarding School. Simon was told how to act at the table but father was far for authoritarian with me. He told me that he was made to hold books under his arms to make sure he didn't stick his elbows out at the dining table. So father put a hard back under each of my arms and I had to hold them there while I eat my diner. If I let one of the books drop father used to pick it up and whack me with the book as hard as he could on the elbow of the arm that I dropped the book from. It would be a regular occurrence for me to have bruises to both elbows. If I was caught chewing food with my mouth open father used to grab a book from under my arm, whack me over the head, then slide the book back under my arm. As I usually dropped the book after being hit on the head I would also get the whack on my arm to go with the one on my head. I would also get whacked on the head with a book if I spoke with food in my mouth and if I didn't respond to a question quickly enough as I had food in my mouth, and I would also get the subsequent whack on the elbow from the book or books that I dropped. I was made to sit and wait for everyone to be seated so we could all start as soon as father started his meal, apart from Simon who could start as soon as he got his plate, sometimes sooner as he would sit at the table picking his nose and eating it.

One thing father was very strict on was saving the meat to eat it last. His reasoning was that if you had to leave anything because I was too full, ill, sent to my room or whatever then the meat could be saved and served up for my next meal.

Chapter 3

I was six when I broke my first bone. On our way home in my father's Mini van, my mother decided to feed my brother Nigel. Nigel was not crying or making a fuss, he was fast asleep. I said to my mother "Please don't feed him now, can't you wait till we get in? Simon Fowler said he saw your boob when you were feeding Nigel the other day." I was really embarrassed being 6 years old, at the time these things were not really done in public. My mother turned round in her seat and hit me with the back of her hand and said "If I want to feed my fucking baby I will and I don't care where I am when I do it!" As my father pulled up in front of the house, my mother lifted her top and undone her bra, exposing both breasts. Nigel was still fast asleep and was not interested in feeding so did not start suckling. My mother got out of the car still with both breasts exposed turned round and said "You're not getting out my side of the fucking car!" and slammed the door closed. My hand was on the door post and when the door slammed shut trapped a couple of my fingers in the door. I screamed with pain. My mother ignored me and walked into the house, still with her top pulled up. My father leaned over and tried to pull me out of the car but as my fingers were trapped in the door, the more he pulled the worse the pain. My other Brother Simon opened the door my side. The relief was immense. I looked at my hand, my fingers were bleeding and my fingers were not pointing straight and I had 2 fingernails missing. My father clipped me round the back of the head and told me to go see my mother and said she would not be happy having to deal with the mess that I'd made. My mother wrapped my fingers in a bit of cotton wool. My little finger was at a strange angle, my mother yanked my fingers together straightening my fingers and then bound them together. I was sent into school the following day with a note explaining that I had "accidentally" got my fingers crushed in a car door. I was sent to the school nurse, she cleaned and dressed my fingers and put a splint between my fingers and bound my little finger to my ring finger. I guess the nurse did a good job as I have not had trouble with these fingers since.

I had a lot of trouble that weekend. Father worked at the local Shell petrol station on the weekends. He usually took me with him as he got me to do all the fetching and carrying. The petrol station was sort of self service but there were some customers who liked to have their petrol put in their car for them. Father used to get me to fill their cars up, he used to be asleep in the office while I was seeing to the customers. Sometimes covering for him was quite hard with how loud he snored. The petrol station owner found out that I was "helping" so he made up a pay packet for me every week. It wasn't much, twenty pence, which was enough to buy a Mars bar a can of drink and a packet of Polo mints, and still have a couple of pence to save.

Father didn't last much longer. All I knew was that he was no longer required and the petrol station closed earlier in the evening. I was sent regularly to the petrol station to buy cigarettes for mother. I was not unusual in those days for kids to be able to buy cigarettes for their parents. "Can I have forty Regal King Size for my mother please?" was the request that was always fulfilled. I never was tempted to try smoking myself and found it disgusting.

Chapter 4

Nigel was not very old, about 6 months, when he was diagnosed with a turn in his eye. He went back and forth to the hospital. Everything stopped for Nigel, if he had an appointment everything else didn't matter. Mind you the Mini Van had gone and was replaced by a Vauxhall Viva, this was an appalling car, it broke down every time it went further than 3 miles. This was typical of my father, buying what he thought was a bargain, but turned out to be junk. The Viva leaked oil and petrol, the electrics were a joke. I'm surprised it didn't catch fire! The state of the car meant that my mother spent a lot of time on a bus taking Nigel to almost every optician in the Vale of Glamorgan. In the end she got her referral for Nigel to the hospital. He was put on the waiting list for an operation to correct the "turn" in his eye. Mother was not happy as she thought he should have the operation immediately.

On one day father came home furious. He had asked one of the mechanics at work to have a look at the Viva. He was told to scrap it as it wasn't worth repairing. Father wanted a price to fix the car and was quoted more than he paid for the car. He decided to do the work himself. I was dragged off to the workshop to "assist" father. Things didn't go to well, and I got shouted at several times for not holding something correctly or not passing a tool quick enough. The final straw was when father tried to remove the sump plug to drain the oil, The nut sheared off, so he took a drill to what was left of the nut. It sort of crumpled under the strain and went inside the sump stripping the treads. Oil went everywhere. "Fuck off home if you're not going to be any use!" was father's rant has he hit me over the head with the oil covered drill. He grabbed the oil catcher as I ran out of the workshop with blood smeared in the oil on my head. When I got home I went straight upstairs and started to wash my hair over the bath. I scrubbed and scrubbed but I could still feel the dirty black oil that smelt very burnt. I felt after washing my hair four or five times that it was as good as it was going to get, so cleaned up the bath and went down stair for a drink.

About an hour later father got home and said "You up the workshops now and clean up that oil!" as I walked past him head down he hit me round the head. I felt the blood trickle down my head. It was not bad but enough to know I was bleeding. When I got to the workshops the first thing I did was clean my head up. I left the bloodied towels in the toilet bin.

The car was still up on the lift and pretty much in the same state as it was when I left. I dragged the bin of spill soil over and used the little shovel to cover the oil. and I then brushed it in and shovelled it in to the dirty bin. Just as I was finishing father came back. He used a cork in place of the sump plug. He hammered it in to make sure it didn't come out, then filled the car up with the oil from the workshop dispenser. He started the car eventually, there was so much smoke thick and acrid. I was glad when he opened the shutter door to drive the car out. It coughed and spluttered in to the yard. I was instructed to close the shuttered door. When I did father said "You can make your own way home as I'm going to pick up your mother."

As I walked home I had to pass a house where an old forestry worker lived. Mr Gather had been retired for years and he had an orchard. He never picked an apple or a pear but they were his pride and joy and spent so much time nurturing them but not enjoy the fruit when it was ready. He would rather it rotted than let anyone else have any. Some of us kids has asked him to sell us some apples, he refused. So as I passed the apples looked so good, I had not eaten that day. Luckily there were a couple of branches hanging over the fence and the fruit were within easy grasp. So I grabbed a few. As I tucked in to the first apple, it was so sweet and juicy, Mr Gather came in to his orchard. He raised his stick and started shouting. I ran with my apples. When I got home I ate them as quickly as I could. Just as I finished Mother and Father walked in the door.

Father hit me over the head, I felt the ooze of blood again but not as bad as before. "Old man Gather stopped me and told me you have been scrumping apples. I've told you before, whatever you get from him, I want some!" "Get caught again and I'll take my belt to you" was his warning

Chapter 5

My father came home with a Labrador Puppy. He was named Honey by my parents. My father bragged how Honey was from Sandylands which he said was where the Queen got her Labradors from. Honey was a bit of a roamer. He got out when he was not very old and cut his ear on barbed wire. My father was furious, not only did he have to pay a vet's bill, it meant Honey could not be shown as he had a large scar on his ear. Honey had to go back several times to have the ear re-stitched as every time the stitches came out, within an hour of coming home his ear would start bleeding heavily. Honey was not very obedient. He did follow me around and was "my" dog. He didn't really pay much attention to anybody else but was not far away from me when I was not at school. I'm sure my father wanted to breed Honey as he saw it as an easy way to make money. Honey however had other ideas, he got a couple of local bitches pregnant but was not interested when he was supposed to perform.

I suppose honey was a free spirit, then again he had no proper disciple at home. My parents had no patients with him and just shouted at him or hit him when he didn't do what they wanted.

On one particular day I was in the playing field playing football with Robert and Simon when honey came running past. He had something in his mouth, so we ran after him. Father was out by the car trying to tinker with it. Honey deposited a rabbit's head at father's feet. "That no fucking good to me" he shouted as he kicked Honey. Where the fuck is the rest of it you greedy bastard?" I pulled honey away from father's kicks and got between them in the process. Father stared to kick me, damn they hurt his steel toe capped boots making contact with my legs. "You'd better teach him how to hunt properly cos if he's going to bring anything home it had better be something I can eat."

I dragged Honey off in to the back garden and sat crying in the corner behind a tree. Honey sat down next to me and licked my face. I felt he knew the pain I was feeling.

Chapter 6

My father was not too good at anything practical. My father always did the least he could to get his car through it's annual MoT. When I was about six or seven I was told to go with my father whenever he was doing any work on the car. I don't know whether this was to keep me out of my mother's hair or not, I felt that my mother could not stand to have me around much of the time. I learned at an early age to read the instructions or manuals. I wasn't allowed to mess around in the workshop. These days I do know how dangerous it is, perhaps something you don't appreciate as a kid. I was told repeatedly that if I hurt myself messing around in the workshop I would not be taken to hospital, and that I would just have to get on with it. Being so young I was bored hanging round watching my father, the only books around were manuals, so I read them. I would be reading the manual as my father was working on the car, watching him bodge the repairs. When I got a little older and mother found out what I was doing while my father was bodging his car, she instructed me to go with my father and ensure he fixed things so that the car passed it's MoT. Then again if the bodges failed as they usually did after a short time, I got the blame, either for not instructing my father what to do or giving him the wrong instructions. I found as I got into my teens it was easier for me to take over and fix the car as per the manual. Then again as I got older I was at home less so was not around when the car needed fixing.

It also meant that whenever my siblings got anything that needed assembly I was usually given orders to do it. Especially at Christmas, I was told to leave my presents alone and sort out whatever needed doing for my siblings. If I protested I was called selfish amongst other things, and was told that I could not touch my presents until my tasks were completed.

One Christmas I had asked for an Action Man, they were all the rage at the time. As usual I got very little, but Simon got an Action Man. It was a sentry post road block and Armoured car. I was not allowed to touch my presents until I had assembled it all. So I assembled it all for him, he just looked at me and threw it in a corner and didn't touch it. About 3 weeks later he took it up to his room and put it in the bottom of his wardrobe. If the Action Man fell out Simon would kick it back in to the wardrobe. It was not long before it was in pieces. Simon would also used the Armoured car to stand on to get stuff from the top of his wardrobe. Again it wasn't long before that was broken too.

Chapter 7

When I was seven we had a new teacher arrived at our Primary School, Mr George. Apparently he was the cousin of a famous Welsh rugby player. Mr George was an accomplished rugby player himself and had played at a high level before going into teaching. So Mr George took over the PE duties for the school. He started a school rugby team for which I was a member of. We were quite successful winning more matches than we lost. I experienced my first broken nose in my first year playing for the school. I remember sitting in the middle of the pitch with blood streaming from my nose, crying. After the match the school nurse sorted me out, and took me to get my nose x-rayed and straightened. When I got home mother was not happy as there was blood all over my kit, which meant that she would have to wash it. Not her strong point. My kit had to wait for a few days and it was getting close to when I was due to play rugby I decided to try washing my rugby kit. It looked simple enough. I got my kit washed although it didn't come out as clean as I'd hoped.

I suppose my rugby kit looked no worse than my school clothes. We didn't have a uniform but my clothes were hand me downs of hand me downs. They were pretty thread bare in places. I tried to hid the places that were worn through. I suppose it didn't matter as I'm sure everybody knew that I had holes in my clothes. I couldn't have Simons shoes as hand me downs as my feet were already as big as his. I got cursed every time I needed shoes.

Chapter 8

When school holidays started we had our first family holiday, a camping trip to Cornwall for two weeks, which my Gran (My father's Mother) paid for. My father acquired a 6 birth tent and trailer. We were all packed in the car including my Gran and off to Cornwall. I spent most of the holiday fetching and carrying. I was not allowed to far in case I was needed. I remember having to stand holding the portable TV's aerial for ages so my mother could watch something on the TV. The second week we stayed in a chalet. My Gran refused to sleep on a camp bed any longer so she paid extra for the chalet. It was a small 2 bedroom affair. My parents had the one room, my Gran the other. Simon had the two seater sofa, Caroline had one chair, Nigel had the other. I slept on the floor. I asked my father if I could have my camp bed but he refused as he had packed it at the bottom of the trailer and he wasn't unpacking the trailer just for my camp bed.

I had always covered up as I had been aware for as long as I could remember that I got sun burnt quite badly. As we were away on holiday I asked mother if she could get some sun protection. "I'm not getting any sun tan lotion for you, you little bastard. I don't need it and neither does your father so I'm not wasting money on you!" From that moment on I knew not to ask again. We went on the beach and mother was doing her usual sun worshiping. She always had leathery skin and loved to sit in the sun. I spent a lot of time in the sea trying to keep cool. However I was wearing a white airtex t-shirt and I got burnt through the t-shirt. I was in a lot of pain and was quite ill with it. All I got from mother was "You'd better not throw up in the car or in the tent. If you do you will sleep outside!" I spent the next few days in the shade. I drank plenty of water as I could get that from the stand pipe, and it didn't cost me anything.

Apart from the day I got sun burnt, shower time on this holiday was not very good for me. My father used to take Simon and myself to the shower room. In those days there were no showers in the chalets either so the same thing happened even when we moved into the chalet. So it was ten pence for five minutes. My father would only put the one ten pence in and Simon always got to go first. By the time Simon had finished the time was just about running out. I would step in and almost immediately the hot water would finish, leaving me with a cold shower. Cold water was free so my father was happy with that. After a couple of days, I took some money with me to the shower. When Simon finished in the shower, I asked my father to put in more money, which he refused. I said I would pay but could he put the money in as I couldn't reach. My father once again refused and told me to hurry up as he wasn't wasting time here with me and that he had better things to do than watch me in the shower.

Chapter 9

What was really strange that year was that I had a birthday party. I didn't ask for one or want one. I was told I was having a birthday party and that was that. I was told that Robert and Simon Fowler were coming as were Neil Beams and David Matthews. I knew Neil and David but didn't really like them, and I certainly wouldn't choose to have them at my birthday party. So there was trifle and fairy cakes sandwiches and the like. The oddest thing was, that the dining table was extended and set up in the living room and once all the food was laid out and everyone was there, we were shut in the living room and told we were not to come out under any circumstances, and mother and father left the room and left us to it. Robert tried the door but said he couldn't open it. After about an hour and a half my parents came in and sent everyone home. It was not a birthday party I enjoyed, or could get away from.

That year for my birthday I got a Timex watch. I liked this I suppose it made me feel grown up. I was told I couldn't have a watch with a second hand though as they were more expensive, and that I should be grateful for what I got. A few days after my birthday, I had to run an errand up to the Forestry Commission workshop where my father worked. When I went into the stores, Mr

Shelby, my father's boss was sat at his desk. He was our next door neighbour. He was a stern looking man but was generally kind. I knew he was a WW2 veteran and had served with the American 5th Army although he was a British soldier. Mr Shelby told people that 75% of the American 5th Army was British and always had to chuckle at that. He used to tell me about some of the things he did in the army, but never discussed any of the battles he had been in. Today was different though. Mr Shelby called me over and said "what have you got there?" he sounded quite angry but not with me. So I showed him my watch and told him it was my birthday. Ok he said you go home now, I said I had a message for my father, Mr Shelby said he would pass the message on, and wrote down the message, as he always did.

That night when my father came home he stormed into the living room where I was having my evening meal, mashed potatoes and gravy, everyone else had liver…yuk! My father came over to me taking his belt off as he came over. He dragged me out of chair, pushed me on the ground and started to hit me with his belt, "You little bastard why did you have to wear that fucking watch to the workshop?" I just curled up and took the lashings. Fortunately for me my father was using the tongue end of the belt as he normally used the buckle end to hit me with. I guess it was what came quickest to his hand.

Father would take a puff of his cigarette before hitting me each time.

Chapter 10

I couldn't wait for the summer holidays to finish, as it meant back to school. At hot meal at lunch time, and a pudding. I did enjoy junior school, I was warm and dry, most of all a good meal at lunch time. The teachers were ok. I got on with Mr George, I always got encouragement from him. I was never directly taught by him, but he took PE and rugby. I always tried my best in PE and was so enthusiastic about rugby. Mr George also set up for us to go to the Hodge Home, a nearby establishment that catered for disabled people. They had a small swimming pool that we used to use. There were links between the Hodge Home and our school. We used to do various fund raising events for the benefit of the Hodge Home. Harvest festivals, summer fetes, Christmas Collections and raffles.

I enjoyed reading and took books from the school library. I suppose it was escapism. I found myself drifting in to the story. I read Reach For The Skies about Douglas Bader. I was in awe of his heroism, how he battled losing both legs in a flying accident but going on to become a fighter ace in the Royal Air force during World War Two. I wanted to read more books about the war, as it was real not like the fiction books. there seemed to be a rawness and reality that the fiction books could not match. I could imagine being there in the story, something that I could not do as easily with the fiction books. I did enjoy the fiction books though. I was a little young and did have trouble understanding some parts. I was glued to the World War Two films that were on the television. They were usually in black and white but that didn't matter to me.

I was not popular with my parents as by the time I went back to school I needed new shoes. They used to take me to Clarks in Cowbridge to get my feet measured then go to the cheapest place to buy shoes. I had no choice in what shoes I had, It was pretty much the cheapest shoes that would fit.

Chapter 11

When Nigel was two he went in for corrective surgery on his eye. The whole world revolved around Nigel, especially now. Nigel was in hospital for a couple of days, but the whole time that Nigel was in hospital mother was snuggled up to him, cuddling him, kissing him. The kind of affection she never showed me. It was almost like she was showing off how much she cared for Nigel and wanted the whole world to know. It was almost perverse the way she was fawning all over Nigel. That was mother all over though, Nigel was the baby, but the type of affection mother showed Nigel, just did not seem natural, not what a mother would or should show her son, it seemed so much more.

Then again if mother was showering Nigel with affection, she was not having a go at me. With mother in the hospital with Nigel, it was everyone for themselves for meal time. It meant I could help myself without mother saying I couldn't have this or that.

Chapter 12

The summer of my eighth birthday (1975) we went to Cornwall again. Once again my Grandmother paid for this holiday but this time she did not come with us. This was to be 2 weeks in the tent. I got to be holder of the television areal again, and once again Simon had a hot shower while I had a cold one. I remember the camp site owner coming over and telling us we would have to leave. There was quite a row and my father refused to pay the bill so we left under a bit of a cloud. We did manage to get another camp site allow us to stay for our second week. Father had to hand over a load of cash before we could stay.

My birthday was at the end of the week, I was told that as we were away on holiday that would be my present from my mother and father that year. I would have to wait and see if I had any cards from anyone else when we got home. If I had cards when we got home I never got them. I usually had money from both my grandmother and my mother's sister. My Mother's mother usually got me something small. But I didn't get anything that year. My mother told me it was because we were on holiday. It was the last family holiday we had.

Our dog Honey was left at home in the passage between the outhouse and the kitchen. When we got back Honey had gnawed a hole in the bottom of the door, his head was poking out to greet us when we got home. I felt really sorry for Honey. He should never have been left at home for that amount of time. I don't know if anybody went in to check on Honey and let him out, but knowing my parents I doubt that anyone went in to sort Honey out. Judging by the amount of dog mess I had to clear up from the passage I doubt that he was let out.

Chapter 13

One outstanding memory of the summer of 1975 when I was eight, and not long after my birthday, and a week or so after we came back from our holiday. My mother always said I was a finicky eater. One day she served me up chopped pork with stuffing from a tin with boiled potatoes for tea. She knew I didn't like the chopped pork and stuffing. I refused to eat it. She made me sit there for the next few hours until bed time. I was served up the same meal for the next 3 days and not allowed to eat anything else until I had eaten the meal that I so despised. Mother sitting at the table to ensure that I either eat it or did not eat anything else. The only time I was able to sneak a drink was when cleaning my teeth morning and night when I snuck a drink from the tap in the bathroom at night or when I went to the toilet I would drink from the tap after washing my hands. On the third day at lunch time there was a knock on the door, mother put the dog in the garden while answering the door. I opened the window and fed the dog the now dried up chopped pork and stuffing and the potatoes. As mother came back in she saw me finish giving the dog my meal through the window. She flew into a rage and started to punch and slap me on my head and face, I fell to the floor so she started to kick me. As I curled up in a ball with blood seeping from cuts on my head, she kicked and stomped me under the table. Screaming at me that as I had fed the dog my food I could eat the dog's food and I could stay under the table like a dog until she said so, and that my father would sort me out when he came home. That night when my father came home just after 5 he dragged me out from under the table by my hair. The next thing I knew I was back on the floor with another mark on my face. I lay there as he took his belt off. He dragged me up off the floor again and bent me over the table, almost ripping off my shorts before he laid into me. I lost count of how many times he gave me six of the best with his belt, not the strap end but the buckle end. It was enough so that I would not be able to sit down for a month of Sundays as he said. It hurt that much I truly believed him. That night it was very difficult to get some sleep. A combination of the physical and emotional pain being excruciating. That was the first time that I considered running away. The only thing stopping me was I hurt so much, I could hardly walk.

Chapter 14

A couple of weeks later my father arrived home with a brand new single bed. One of the many back handers he received as his job as Senior Storeman for South Wales for the Forestry Commission. I was given the brand new bed, his reasoning for giving it to me was my elder brother Simon still was wetting the bed. Perhaps he was right, but I still had bruises and cuts healing. My parents told me I was lucky that I was on school summer holiday or I would have a lot of explaining to do to the school as to why I was in such a state. Nothing was said but I knew not to say anything or there would be more of the same.

A week before school started after the summer holiday, my brother pushed me over in the front room. As I fell I caught my eye brow on the corner or the dining table. A cut of about 4 inches or so opened up and it was really deep. I had never seen so much blood. I could not see out of my left eye there was so much blood. I grabbed a towel and held it to my eye to try and stop the bleeding. Mother came over shouting what have I done calling me stupid for doing something like that. She slapped me round the head and said that if I thought I was going to hospital to have it looked at I could think again as she wasn't sitting up there for hours. It took quite a while for the bleeding to stop. Over the next few days every time I bumped the cut it would ooze blood.

A few days later it was the start of autumn term. I was sent to the school nurse just after registration. She was nice and ironically called Mrs Nurse. Mrs Nurse asked me how I cut my eye, I told her my brother pushed me and I hit the corner of the dining table. She cleaned it up, that should have been stitched she said, at least 6 maybe 8 stitches. Why didn't you go to hospital? She asked. Well my mother used to be a nurse so she saw to it I said. It was the standard family response when anything like that happened. It was only years later that I found out my mother never completed her training as a nurse and was kicked out of nursing in her first semester of training. It was a good job Mrs Nurse didn't ask to take my shirt off, I still had bruising over my body, even though it was quite faded.

Then again I suppose it would not have taken much to remove my shirt, there wasn't much left to it, as it was a hand me down of a hand me down, as we most of my clothes. When I got in from school I made a cup of tea, something that I enjoyed from an early age. My mother went nuts, saying that as I drunk so much milk in my tea, then I would have to buy my own milk and tea. The milk man delivered every other day, and my mother insisted that I pay for one pint out of the six we had delivered. My mother would round up the cost of "my" milk every week, I would end up paying for 1 extra pint. My mother's argument was that if I didn't like it, I could walk to the nearest shop which was two miles away and buy my own milk. When I made tea I usually made a small pot that held about two cups worth of tea. If I left the room for any reason, on my return my cup would be empty. I found that I liked tea without sugar. Funnily enough my tea was left alone after that.

Chapter 15

One Friday evening we went on our usual shopping trip to Leos in Cardiff. My father would travel to Cardiff to save a few quid on the shopping bill, however he probably used more in petrol than he saved on the shopping. This trip was different, Honey came with us. Honey sat in the footwell in front of me. Honey had been having some fits in the last few months, he was a little grumpy and I suppose disorientated when the fit was over. I was the only one who could go near him after a fit. His mood improved once he had recovered from the fit, but he was having 2 or 3 fits a week. So this Friday we were dropped off at my Gran's house. About an hour later my mother and father came back to pick us up, but no Honey. "Where's Honey?" I asked. "He was a nasty bastard after his fits so we've had him put down!" was mother's spiteful scorn. I was heartbroken, Honey and I did loads together, I was sure there was something that could be done for him. I had been to the vets with Honey when the fits got more regular. The local vet said it was epilepsy which would mean Honey would have to take medicine for the rest of his life. My father's instant response was "I'm not paying for that." Mother said "Honey was to inter bread which turned him into a nasty bastard." He might have been to mother but never to me or the kids I hung around with. "You are both murderers!" I shouted at my parents. "You just didn't want to pay for his medicine. MURDERERS!" Bam mother's right hand connected with face with such force that it knocked me to the ground. I shouted "Murderer" each time mother hit me. My Gran came out of her kitchen "That's enough!" she told my mother. "He didn't deserve that." I was surprised that my Gran had stood up for me. Mother went silent and turned round and walked out to the car. My father herded us kids out to the car. "I don't want to hear a sound" Was father's order as we drove home.

Chapter 16

That Christmas was a big surprise for me, I had a pair of binoculars for my Christmas present. I enjoyed bird watching, and the binoculars were a good start. The binoculars were cheap and 8 x 40, another work freebee. In the New Year my father came home and said he had spoken to the Forestry Commission Nursery manager and he wanted me to find out how many birds of prey there were on the Forestry Commission land at Tair Onen. I spent days watching various birds and making notes on what I had seen. I made a nice neat chart of what I had seen and where and gave it to the Nursery manager. He was really pleased. "Thanks Clive, I'll give your dad your money for doing this when I see him. Is that ok? I don't have any money on me now." I was surprised by this statement, my father said nothing about money, and I never did see it though.

A couple of days later my sister was running around in her knickers in the front room. She was generally being a pain. She picked up my binoculars and was teasing me with them, going to give them to me then pulling away. I said to mother that Caroline had my binoculars and wouldn't give them back. Mother told me to shut up and stop bothering her. Caroline was still trying to tease me, but I was too quick for her and grabbed my binoculars. She lunged at me and I put my hand up. She took a half step backwards, however Simons favourite thing at the time was tripping people up who stepped backwards or walked backwards. Caroline tripped and nearly fell on the hearth of the fire. I guess her backside got a little warm but nothing more. Luckily I grabbed her as she fell and pulled her away. Simon was in fits of laughter.

Mother wasn't though. She said it was all my fault and grabbed the poker that she had just used to poke the fire. She swung it and it hit me on the calf the first time and my backside the second and third time. Lucky for me it had lost most of it's heat. She yelled at me to "Get the fuck out of my sight, piss off to bed!" No dinner for me that night. I guess I was getting used to it.

The following morning I was starving and I was up early but I didn't have time for breakfast though. I was going with father to pick up his Aunt Vera from Luton Airport, and I had to map read. It looked an easy route to me, down the M4, round the North Circular and then off to Luton. Father stopped at Leigh Delamare services and had something to eat from the restaurant. There wasn't anything that I liked on the menu. I thought I'd get something from the shop on the way out, father had other ideas, he said he wasn't hanging around waiting for me to make up my mind, and wasn't wasting his money on sweets.

He didn't have chocolate as a kid growing up during the war so didn't see why I needed it now.

When we got on the North Circular Road, there were lots of traffic lights. After several sets of traffic lights an E Type Jaguar pulled up alongside us. Immediately father saw this as a challenge. As soon as the lights turned green father screeched off leaving the E Type behind foot hard on the accelerator and not lifting even to change gear. He used to call this his racing change that he had been taught by a mate of his, in reality father didn't lift the accelerator pressed the clutch and rammed the gear leaver into each gear. At the next couple of traffic lights the same thing happened, father was in ecstasy. He was so pleased his Ford Cortina Mark II 1600e was faster than and E Type Jaguar and he was a better driver. Thing is the driver of the E Type was not even trying, he was just pulling away normally and he seemed amused at father trying so hard to get ahead, only for father to have to slam on the brakes at the next traffic lights. The E Type turned right after the fifth set of lights and we didn't see him again.

We arrived in time to pick up Auntie Vera. When she met us she gave father her luggage, he immediately passed it to me, all four suitcases. Auntie Vera had been to Australia for a few months to visit her daughter. this was the first time I had met her and she seemed a very stern mean bitter old lonely woman. Father shepherded her towards the car as I carried the luggage. Father had a boot full of stuff so the suitcases had to go in the back with me. We stopped on the way back at the same service station. I had to stay in the car to make sure the luggage was safe. When father and Auntie Vera came back suitably refreshed I asked if they brought me anything, father said he forgot. He turned to Auntie Vera and said, "He'll be alright, he'll feel sick soon enough and won't feel like eating." Father then proceeded to light his pipe which he knew made me feel so ill. He was right though soon I was feeling too sick to feel hungry.

Once we dropped Auntie Vera off at Gran's house as she was moving in we went home. As soon as we got in father started to tell tales of how he out dragged an E Type Jaguar at EVERY set of traffic lights. Father used to bring out this tale every so often. It wasn't long before this car was broken due to father's rough driving style. The gearbox broke, and that was another car that hit the dust. It was laid up for weeks while father decided what to do with it. In the end father decided to sell his pride and joy as it was too expensive to fix.

Chapter 17

Over the next two years I did as much as I could to stay out of the way. I still got beaten regularly, even if I had done nothing wrong, just to keep me inline. The one thing I could not understand, my father made a big deal of being a Roman Catholic, but every Sunday we were shipped off to Sunday School at the local prespetarian chapel for a couple of hours. We had a mini bus come and collect us and drop us off afterwards. Now don't get me wrong the people there were nice, and a couple of the kids were friendly, but I never could understand why we were shipped off there every Sunday when my father was supposed to be a Catholic and whenever we were asked my father said we were Catholic. If the family was that religious why didn't my parents go to church? Looking back it just seems like we were wanted to be out of the way. For what I can only imagine. We were at this time shipped off to my Aunt's on my father's side every Friday night and was picked up Sunday morning, just in time to get home to be picked up by the bus to take us to Sunday School. At least while I was there it meant that I was treated equally to everyone else. No beatings or verbal abuse. I had some good food to eat too! I suppose I frustrated my Aunt too. Just before we used to go out I would always want a drink or go to the toilet which would set the rest of the kids off as well, and as there were nine of us kids, I guess it was frustrating. My Aunt always used to comment on how I was always trying to keep myself clean and took extra care in cleaning my shoes. Something which I suppose is a little odd for a young child, but when you look at the state of the house that I grew up in I suppose it's not surprising. What is surprising is that I didn't grow up with OCD, then again I did like to do a lot of the other things kids did, like sport.

That spring the Forestry Commission entered a float in the Cowbridge Carnival. the first I heard of it was the morning of the carnival. The float was brought to the street and was a flat bed lorry that was decorated as a teddy bear's picnic. Mother got quite excited. I was told to dress in a shirt and short trousers. When I got outside it was quite chilly and it was drizzling and raining and quite a blustery wind. I tried to go back in to the house, Mother said "Where do you think you are going?" I'm going to put my trousers on and get a coat" was my reply. "No you don't get back here!" was her order, I was bundled on to the lorry and give a teddy bear mask. Simon appeared late as usual, he was wearing his trousers and he had a jumper on. "Why can't I get a jumper and my long trousers like Simon?" "Too late your going now and you don't have time." was mother's retort. The drive to Cowbridge was awful I got soaked and was freezing. When we got to the staging area, some of the other kids from the estate arrived. We had to wait for about two hours before the parade started. Mother would not let me off the lorry, not even to go to the nearby toilet.

Finally we were told we were about to start, all the other kids had coats or macs on. The driver got in and started the lorry up. Mother came to the side of the lorry where I was sitting. "Clive over here" was her order. I leant over the side of the lorry, "Lift your mask for a second!" was her order As I did so the back of her right hand caught me on the side of my mouth, her ring opening up a little cut. "You fuck this up for me and that will be the least of your worries! Now go and sit the fuck down and wave to the crowd when you are supposed to!" was her order as she place the mask back over my face. She made sure she said it quietly so as not for other people to hear.

I sat back down, when the parade turned in to the main street I waved as I was told to. The parade was slow and at walking pace so it took time for us to get to the area where the carnival finished. When we arrived one of the Forestry workers and a few of the parents brought food on to the lorry. There was a table in the middle. There were sandwiches sausage rolls scotch eggs crisps loads of soft drinks as well as sweets and deserts. I sat in the corner and tried not to be noticed. I didn't take my mask off as I didn't want anyone to see my split lip. When the feast was over mother came over and called Simon and told him to get off the lorry. I went to get off and all I got was "You can stay here!" When it was finally over the driver returned and said he told my father he would drop me off if he wanted as he had to drop the lorry off. Father agreed. I was allowed to sit in the cab on the way home, at least it was warm and dry in there. The driver was pretty chatty but I didn't say much on the way home. I thanked the driver and got out of the lorry. When I got home the house was dark and cold. I boiled the kettle and made a cup of tea. with the rest of the water I used to have a strip wash. I fell asleep really quickly and didn't hear everyone else come in until the bedroom light was turned on and Simon made loads of noise coming in. Father carried Nigel into the bedroom and dumped him on his bed. It took an hour for Simon to stop being noisy and turn the light out. That night I dreamed of being with another family.

Chapter 18

The summer of 1976 was the longest and hottest on record in this country. I must admit I did feel healthier than I ever had done before. I felt happy in the sunshine. Being a long hot and dry summer and my father being in the Forestry Commission meant there were record forest fires and that meant almost every worker was on fire fighting duty. We hardly saw my father from May until October. We did have workmen on the estate putting in new wiring in all the houses. Some of us kids on the estate decided to pick on them and have water fights with them during their lunch break. Water was pretty rationed as there was a drought and water shortage. Water was turned on by the water company at night but was off during the day. So we would fill up old washing up liquid bottles, they held a lot more water than the water pistols of the day. There was a local lake that we spent a lot of time at, but we did not go swimming in the lake. There were rumours of big pike in the lake, and being young impressionable kids we were told of pike that eat dogs and swans lived in the lake. I never saw any pike though. There was a stream that runs into the lake but the other end there was a bridge and a small waterfall about two to three feet tall that the water exited the lake. That was a great place to be when it was so hot.

During the summer all the houses were being rewired. It must have been quite hard work in the heat. The workmen were very friendly. They were good fun too. We did have water fights between us kids. I cannot remember how but the workmen got involved. I was no contest really, four of us kids against two workmen. They ended up locked in their van. However it was too hot to close their vents, even though they closed their windows. We soon worked out that we could still soak them through the open vents. It was the most fun I had that summer. In fairness the workmen knew they were beat and took it in good fun, then again it was so hot, it must have been a welcome distraction from the heat. These water fights happened quite regularly when the workmen were on their lunch break. We did not stop the workmen from doing their jobs; we only started the water fights during their breaks. There was water rationing so we used to fill up buckets and our water pistols at night when the water was on, as the water was off during the day. Then my mother found out what was happening. She went ballistic, we were wasting water. When I said the Fowler boys were playing, my mother said she didn't care what they did. I got the usual "if they jumped off a bridge, would I do the same?" I got whacked with the bamboo that was by the fire in the front room. But I was able to slip the blows so they didn't hurt that much. I was told to get out of my mother's sight, which I did. The water that we used for the water fights was what we collected just for that purpose and we didn't take any of the water that was used for household needs, we got some extra buckets and only used the water that we collected in these buckets. All the houses had massive water tanks in their lofts so when the water was switched off during the day, it was very rare for anyone to run out of water. Mind you in our house water wasn't used much for washing of any kind.

I know a lot of the men that worked in the workshop that my father worked in were loaded with all the overtime that they put in. There were lots of new cars on our estate some had foreign holidays, new televisions and such things. We did not get anything new. Although that year I got a bike for Christmas, my brother Simon got a Raleigh Chopper, which was all the rage at the time, I got a cheap push bike.

Chapter 19

When February came I went into hospital to have my tonsils and adenoids removed. I had been on the waiting list for five year so my mother told me to have this operation. I did suffer with tonsillitis many times a year. When I was in hospital the food was great, I ate most of the food that was served up. The fact that I was under weight was highlighted but my mother was insistent that this was down to tonsillitis that I had suffered repeatedly. Hospital was Ely ENT in Cardiff. There were two wards in this department, pre and post operative wards. I had a bed midway down the pre operative ward. No one told me what would happen. I was admitted early morning the day before the operation, so I was there for breakfast. So I had three hearty meals that day. I had examinations blood tests height weight blood pressure and all the usual things done to me to prepare me for the operation. The following morning I was up and washed ready for breakfast. However, when breakfast didn't arrive I was disappointed but not surprised. Mid morning I was really thirsty, I had been playing and not thought about a drink until then. There were no jugs of water or glasses. So I asked the nurse if I could have a drink and she said no, so I went to the sink and turned on the tap. The nurse had to pull me away from the tap to stop me drinking from it. "Didn't your mother tell you that you couldn't have a drink today?" I said "No, why?" The nurse sat down with me and explained about the anaesthetic and why I couldn't have anything to eat or drink before the operation, but that when I recovered and was up to it I could have something soft to eat after the operation and a drink. Ok so I understood. The nurse was not happy and said that she would get Sister to have a word with my mother when she came in. Later that morning I was taken away for my operation. I was given a pre med an hour before and was quite sleepy when they took me away, the last thing I remember was being on the trolley on the way to the theatre. The next thing I remember was coming round in the post operative ward. I was allowed to have small sips of water. The evening meal would be round later. Visiting time started, but my parents were late. Every other child in the ward had visitors. Half an hour later my parents turned up. As they were walking in the ward I coughed. That's when the problems started. I coughed again, this time blood coming out of my mouth, blood started to pour out of my mouth. A nurse was near my bed and saw what was happening. The nurse immediately came over called for help and hit the emergency button above my bed. I was told to lie down and to try and swallow the blood. I did lie down, and swallow the blood by kept on being sick with the blood that I had swallowed. There were nurses and doctors everywhere doing this and that, sticking me with needles. My mother came over and tried to take over, trying to be the centre of attention. A sister came over with a bag of blood, she knew my mother and said hello. My mother was still trying to direct everything. The sister turned to my mother and said "Look Gill you are in the way, shut up and sit down over there!" it wasn't a request, it was the first time I had heard someone bark orders at my mother and my mother do as she was told without any argument. I was sick several times, bringing up the blood I had swallowed. Each time I brought up the blood it filled a metal kidney dish. I must admit I was scared, but at the same time I was at peace and calm. I didn't have any thoughts of dying just what will be will be. I was rushed off for emergency surgery. When I returned later that night, visiting time was over and my parents had gone. The next morning the doctors did their rounds. The doctor who seemed to be in charge came over to me and said "let's go and sit down over here." We went and sat down on the kids table. The ward sister joined us. The doctor and the sister explained to me what happened. They explained that I had ruptured an artery in my throat and lost a lot of blood. I had to have a blood transfusion of 4 units, and that the surgery and the transfusion had saved my life. They both explained that as my throat was delicate due to the surgeries I had to eat soft food for a month until it healed. They wrote down a list of food that I should be eating, soft cereal for breakfast like porridge, mashed potatoes and fish or soup for lunch, and anything soft for diner. I had the mashed potato and fish with parsley sauce for lunch, with ice cream and jelly to follow. My parents were late in for visiting only making the last half hour. A nurse came over and informed my parents that I would be going home in the morning and that I would be ready about 10. The nurse also said that the sister wanted to have a word with my parents but she had finished her shift and waited around for an hour of visiting time but had to go. When the nurse left my mother said to my father, "old friend from when I was a nurse, I bet she wants to catch up. We'll have to be here tomorrow at Ten." The next morning I was ready to go home, with a full tummy after a nice bowl of porridge for breakfast. The doctors were there when my mother came in and gave her instructions for my after care and what food I needed and after care. Mother was informed that I would have a follow up appointment in two weeks and then another two weeks after that at my GP. When the doctors left and as the rest of the parents and children were leaving, the sister came over and said "Can I have a word?" It didn't seem like a request more like a demand. My mother was all smiles, "Of course you can." The Sister explained that she thought I was a victim of abuse and that if she found any proof she would have no hesitation in calling the police. The Sister explained that she would be checking that I had everything that was required for my recovery and that I would have the type and quantity of food that the doctors had decided that I needed. If she found out that I didn't get what I needed for my recovery, then she would be reporting me to the Police. My mother was not best pleased.

I was taken home and I had good meals that day, but I was meant to feel guilty about it. "You do realise while you are eating that stuff, the rest of us have to go short?" was my mother's scornful remark. Mind you it did not seem the rest of the family was going short. Then again it meant my father didn't have steak that week, just pork chops. The day after I came home the district nurse came to visit. She told me that the ward sister had asked her to visit me and she would every couple of days. That afternoon, my mother was brought home by her boss, a Mr Lawrence Bunn. He came in to see me with some ice cream. Mr Bunn said "This is for you and only you, I heard what happened, I hope you get well soon." Raspberry ripple ice cream is still my favourite, and twice a week for the next 3 months Mr Bunn sent a two litre tub of raspberry ripple ice cream. Mr Bunn would also ask every time I saw him if I had enjoyed the ice cream and he also asked if only I had eaten the ice cream as he had given it to me for my recovery not for anyone else to pig out on it.

Chapter 20

One Saturday stuck out not long after having my tonsils out. We went to my Grandmother's (Father's mother) while my parents supposedly went food shopping. when they collected us kids, we got our coats on ready to go. Mother turned to me and said "Have you washed behind your ears? Go and wash them NOW!" So off I went washed my face and behind my ears. When I came back down mother went off on one. "You dirty little bastard you haven't bothered washing behind your ears now go and do it properly!" Off I went again. When I returned the response was pretty much the same, as was the third time. The fourth time I was sent up to wash behind my ears, I took a scrubbing brush and scrubbed behind my ears with Ajax powder. My Grandmother past the bathroom where I was scrubbing my ears and asked me what I was doing so I told her, she came down stairs with me. As soon as I got down stairs, mother started "You haven't cleaned behind your ears properly, you little liar!" My grandmother said "Shut up, he's been up there with a scrubbing brush and Ajax, so don't have a go at him for having dirty ears but he hasn't." Mother left with a face like thunder. We could hear the car door slam as she got in from inside the house.

Just as we got home mother turned round and said "Got your Gran to hide behind, you won't be able to hide behind her forever!"

Over the next few weeks mother used to taunt me with "You haven't got your Gran to hide behind now." It put me on edge and I was always wondering what was coming next. Mother seemed to take great delight in saying this and seeing my reaction. Sometimes she used to come right up close to my face and say it, and other time she would whisper it in my ear and have a little chuckle when she moved away.

Chapter 21

Later that year, one Saturday my brother Simon was riding his blue plastic tractor indoors and drove into the front door, breaking one of the five panes of glass that made up the front door. My father put us in the car and drove us into Barry to a glass place he knew. He proceeded to order the glass and would take a couple of days.

The following Saturday we went off to Barry as the glass had arrived. We got in to the glaziers and they brought the glass out, father reached for his pocket and patted around his trousers before he said that he had forgotten his wallet, he turned to me and said that he knew I had money so I would have to pay for it. I pulled out a £5 note which I had kept from my birthday. That was the last that I saw of that.

 So we got home and my father got on with fixing the new pane of glass into the door. He called me to give him a hand. As I walked to the front door the new glass was on the floor. I did not see it and trod on it, cracking it. My father flew into a rage. The claw hammer that he was using to pull out the retaining nails from the door hit me right in the side, and flew out of his hand. He threw me up the stairs hitting me and punching me all the way, and telling me that I would have to pay for a new pane of glass for being so stupid.

Later that night father came to my bed room and demanded the money for the glass. I told him that I had paid for that glass so he owed me money. I said it wasn't my fault he put the glass on the floor and that it was his fault. He told me to shut up and pay up or I knew what would happen. I said I had no more money as he had the last of my birthday money for the first pane of glass and kept the change so I had nothing to give him. He said that mother would make me pay one way or another.

Chapter 22

A couple of months later after the front door had been repaired, we were waiting to go out to pick up mother from work. Simon was taunting me so I lashed out with a wild swinging left hook aimed at his ribs. I missed him but I did not miss the front door, I put my fist through the glass. My father grabbed a towel and wrapped my hand up and bundled us into the car. We drove straight to mother's work.

When we got to mother's work she was outside with her boss. He seemed more concerned than mother and after looking at my cut hand insisted that my father take me to A & E. Mother always the caring type decided that as she would have to be back in work two hours later for her next shift, she would not go with us to the hospital. So after 5 hours and a couple of stitches at St David's Hospital in Cardiff I was allowed to go home. First thing that my father said when I got in the car, "I hope you've got enough money to pay for the glass that you broke."

So the following weekend after relieving me of another £5 my father disappeared for a while supposedly to go and get the glass. He came back with a piece of hard board and explained that he had to order the glass so was making the door safe. Mind you to this day the glass has not been replaced.

Mother insisted my father take me to the doctor's to have the stitches removed. "I don't have the time or the inclination to sit down the doctors for ages so you can have your stitches out. You did this to yourself so it's nothing to do with me." was mother's scorn.

Chapter 23

At the start of the new school year Robert started at Comprehensive School. He started running a lot. Robert asked me to run with him. I guess he wanted a training partner, then again Robert always did like to beat people at whatever he was doing and I suppose that being 2 years younger I was easy for him to beat at that stage.

I did enjoy watching the athletics on the television. Steve Ovett was my running hero. He just seemed so genuine, where Seb Coe gave the appearance of being upper class and an air of being better than everyone else. I suppose it was another way to escape from the situation in the house. The scenery is really good where we ran. We had a route that we used to run. It was an ideal place to escape in your thoughts, day dreaming while I was running that I would be running and winning the big race was a regular occurrence. It was a great place to be. Until the reality of getting back to the house at the end of the run, that was. Robert was usually waiting for me when I finished, he was stretching and I used to do the same. I didn't care that he was quicker than me, he was two years older after all but Robert seemed to take some satisfaction out of beating me, he didn't care that it wasn't a fair race, not only was Robert older he had decent running kit, I just had a pair of cheap hand me down road slapper daps and hand me down shorts and t-shirt, but I was not bothered, I enjoyed the freedom of running.

This Christmas we had a Christmas play, the Wizard of OZ. I was to play the head munchkin and I had a singing solo. However, although I was told I had a good voice it was not loud enough so I would have the rest of the munchkins sing along with me although I would have the lead. Rehearsals were as I would think any rehearsals. We had dress rehearsals, and finally the night came. So we had a little face paint on and were in our costumes, I was waiting by my classroom all ready for the play to begin. Mother came down, she looked at me "Hmmm there's something missing." she said and then she grabbed my face with her left hand and put lipstick on me using her right hand, and walked off laughing. At the end of corridor Simon and father. Simon was laughing, "Ha ha Clive's going to look like a girl on stage." All three were laughing. I was trying to rub the lipstick off. Mrs Baker our teacher and the director of the play saw me, she asked what happened, I just shrugged my shoulders. and looked down. Mrs Baker told me not to worry everything would be alright. Come show time I was pretty glum and shuffled up to our starting points still looking at the ground. The introduction music started I looked up briefly. What I saw totally surprised me was everybody has lipstick on. Mrs Baker gave me a big smile as I went on stage. When mother father and Simon realised everybody had lipstick on the look of delight changed. After the play had finished I went and got changed and scrubbed and scrubbed my face and my lips, anything to make sure I got that awful lipstick off. It was very quiet on the way home, there was a bit of an atmosphere. No one said anything and I didn't ask. When I got home I went upstairs cleaned my teeth cleaned and scrubbed my face again and went to bed.

Chapter 24

I think that my father was one of the laziest people I have ever come across. From when I was small we had a large garden. Quite a bit of the garden was taken up with vegetable production. When it came to cultivating the land my father was good at getting myself and my older brother to dig the veggie patch over every year. My father told us what to plant and where to plant it. We were also given instruction on composting and weeding. We did get a decent crop every year, and my father used to boast on how well his garden was growing and how HE worked so hard on it, when in reality he did very little.

When I was ten my father was given a petrol rotavator (Another work freebee) and this was the only time he cultivated the ground. He was never one for manual labour. If you listened to him though, he would be superman! My father also gave my brother and I a small part of the garden each to grow our own veggies. I grew carrots lettuce and radishes. Although my father seemed to think all I grew was radishes for some reason. I must admit for how much veggies we grew, we didn't consume anywhere near that amount. We should have been fairly self sufficient with our vegetable growth but we were always buying vegetables from supermarkets or our local farm shops. As I got older and was not around the house so much doing the various sports and hobbies, the interest in the veggie patch waned. The more that was left to my father to do by himself, the less that actually got done. Father cut the lawn about twice a year. Both times he used a big industrial self propelled lawn mower that he had acquired from the Forestry Commission.

That summer father had a trailer full of manure delivered by a local farmer. The farmer drove up the lane next to the house. Father had come home at lunch time to tell the farmer where to park. Once the farmer had parked up he turned the tractor off. Father turned to him and said "Cuppa?" and off they went. "Clive that needs shovelling in to the compost heap!" it was an order not a request. So I spent the next couple of hours shovelling manure over the hedge on to the compost heap. When I was done I smelled pretty bad. I went to have a bath, but as usual the coal fire wasn't lit as it was summer so no hot water. I still had to have a bath though, even if it was cold. I spent ages in the bath scrubbing myself until I could no longer smell the manure. When I got out I put my clothes in the washing machine. It was still on when mother came home. "Who's washing is in the fucking machine?!" was her demand. "Mine" was my reply. "So why didn't you put some of the other washing in the machine or are too selfish to do anyone else's washing.?" "I got covered in manure shovelling it off the trailer in to the compost heap, so I thought it would be better not to wash those clothes with anyone else's." "Well you could have washed everyone's clothes twice, unless you are too selfish. As you're so selfish you can do your own washing from now on, and if you think your using my washing powder you can think again, now fuck off out of my sight." as I slunk past mother she hit me over the head with something hard. My head was spinning and I could see a few stars. I made my way upstairs. I stayed there for the rest of the evening, and felt a little sick.

A few days later father came home with a what he called a flame thrower. It was like a fat broom handle. It got filled with paraffin and there was a pump at the top that was used to pressurise it and you lit the other end. It was designed for burning weeds and the like. Father used to burn large areas of the vegetable plot instead of weeding it. I heard Mr Fowler saying that it would not last long with father because he was not using it as intended and he treated it badly. Needless to say Mr Fowler was right.

Chapter 25

At ten after a particularly bad beating, I was sent out of the house as mother didn't want to see my face. My crime the cat had messed on the floor. Mother was good at beating me either around the body, or if it was six of the best time it would be the bamboo cane across the back of the hand. If it was six of the best it was six strikes across both hands. She used to take great delight in getting my father giving me six of the best until I cried, and I kept on getting them until I cried, if she thought I was faking it I got even more. So after getting sent outside, I bumped in to Robert and Simon. I said I was going to hide. They didn't know why and thought it was fun, so we went to the woods at the end of our street. We climbed the trees and hid in the canopy. My brother Simon tagged along. I saw my father drive off to take my mother to work. By the time he came back half an hour later it was dark. Robert and Simon's parents were out looking for them. They thought it was funny hiding. My father started to shout at us to come home. My brother went home pretty soon telling my father and Robert and Simon's father where we were. Thing is though the trees we so closely packed together we were able to move from tree to tree with ease. Most of the street was out now beckoning for us to come down. After about an hour Robert and Simon had lost interest and went home, welcomed by their parents. I wasn't ready to home just yet, besides I had one trick up my sleeve. I moved from tree to tree until I got to the far edge, climbed down over the garages across the track at the side of our house and into our garden via the back fence. I snuck into the outhouse. A few minutes later my father came in to the outhouse looking for a torch, and found me there. I thought all hell was going to unleash. He asked me what I was doing there. I explained that I got sent out by mother and although I did climb a tree with the others I returned home and stayed in the outhouse when I saw him drive off to take mother to work. I was both surprised and relieved that he believed what I said. Then again he never was the brightest bulb in the box.

A few days later was my birthday. I had asked for the 1978 world cup football. As usual I didn't get it. However, I did get enough birthday money to buy the ball myself. I bugged father to take me in to Cowbridge to the sports shop. Eventually he was going in to Cowbridge so he said he would drop me off. I was really pleased to buy the ball. However I was not pleased that I had to walk home. As I got about half way home, I heard a horn beep. As I turned I saw father in the car. I felt a little relief at the thought of getting a lift the rest of the way home. Father waved as he drove past.

When I got home father was laughing with mother. "You should have seen his face, when I drove past him." roared father. They both laughed, "I wish I could have seen the stupid little bastard's face." mother howled "Would have been a fucking picture."

Simon came in and inquired what all the fuss was about. Needless to say he joined in.

I stormed out of the room. As I left I heard mother saying "Ha ha look at that face like thunder, little bastard." I could hear all three laughing.

Whenever I played football with the Fowler brothers, Simon was not invited. If Simon did turn up and want to play I would take my ball and not let him play with my ball and go home. Mind you Simon was rubbish and rarely played football anyway.

Chapter 26

Nigel acquired the nick name Ern. This stemmed from Morecombe and Wise comedians from the 70s. My father had a manager who he didn't like whose name was Ernie but he was short and had a complex about his height. Eric Morecombe's catch phrase was "Hello little Earn" while wiggling his glasses. Father worked on Nigel for weeks to get him to do this. So when this manager Ernie went into where my father worked he had Nigel there, and when Ernie's name came up Nigel sprung into his "Hello little Ern" routine. The name stuck with Nigel and some of the locals called him Little Ern from then on.

Mr Fowler brought a pony home one day from his family farm. I think it could stay there any longer so to keep it in the family he brought the playing field. Nigel showed some interest so Mr Fowler put him on the pony's back and he seemed to enjoy it. My Father who was all show to other people so had to appear to go one better although in practice he never did, and people knew what he was trying to do but were not really bothered to say anything.

So Riding lessons were booked for Nigel, Caroline and Simon. I wasn't really interested and surprise, surprise I was left out of any family activity as every activity was worked around the riding. My father went and brought a horse called Duke. Duke was delivered to our home and Duke was placed in our back garden. Duke seemed rather wild and definitely spooked by the travelling. Duke tore up the garden and constantly tried to escape. So after a few days father found a field to put Duke in. So feed was brought and it took another couple of weeks to sort everything out.

My Father decided that as I was the best at getting up in the morning I would have to get him up so he could take me to feed Duke every morning, before school. So I was up at 5.30 every morning get the feed ready and then wake up my father. Once back from feeding Duke I then had to make father a coffee and cook him some bacon and eggs. I used to make the most of this as this was usually the only time I had something decent to eat at home. My father always said he couldn't eat breakfast as it made him sick, but once we got back from feeding Duke he would be first for his fry up. Mind you he still took a sandwich box full of food for his 10 o'clock breakfast and then have lunch at 12 o'clock.

Chapter 27

Once Duke was settled in it was time to have his hooves shod. To save a couple of pounds my father decided to walk Duke the 3 ½ miles to the farrier. However, he needed to have someone ride Duke and that task was left to me as my siblings were at the stables where they had lessons helping out. So off we went, I had never ridden before and Duke was a little skittish to say the least. We got to the common just before the farrier's and my father let go and slapped Duke on the behind. It was not long before I was on the floor. It was a good job there was another rider on the common that day to catch Duke. My mother who had come with us was not amused. As soon as the other rider was out of site after returning Duke she hit me across my back 6 times with the riding crop she was carrying. The shoeing didn't take long and we were soon on our way home.

We were nearly home when a tractor came the other way. The driver seemed to be in a hurry as he was revving the tractor to try and get past. Duke reared up and once again I fell off. Mother told me I would not embarrass her again and I would have lessons weather I liked it or not. Well I was allowed to walk home the couple of minutes walk while Duke was put away by my parents.

Chapter 28

As I was now taking riding lessons I was volunteered to be a helper at the stables. This meant being out of the house by 7.00 AM Saturday and Sunday. This happened regardless or weather and regardless of any illness or injuries I had. It was almost like slave labour. We were neither paid nor had any other reward. Once I was competent enough on a horse then I'd be very lucky to get a working ride as a helper on a teaching ride. More likely was to walk along side a learner rider holding the lead reign. It wasn't pleasant work at times, with mucking out of the stables, grooming the horses cleaning tack and all the other chores that go along with working at a riding stables. Mind you I did have a riding "lesson" paid for by my parents. So I got to ride at least once a weekend. Then again as long as I was doing as they wanted life was fairly peaceful. It meant that I kept out of their way. However, my parents had never taken such an interest in any of my hobbies or pastimes. Then again they never spent the time up the stables with us kids or riding but in the company of the stable owner. I can only guess as to why. Thinking back there was always lewd comment made by father to Margret, mother encouraged him and laughed at his comments.

Chapter 29

During my last year at Maendy County Primary School I did my cycling proficiency test. I had to ride my bike the 4 miles down narrow country lanes to school, as my father said he would not take my bike as I was quite able to ride my bike to school. The other kids on our little estate had their bikes taken to school on the Monday Morning in one of the Forestry Commission's Land Rovers. When my father was asked if he wanted to have my bike taken to school, he refused. We had a week of being taught how to ride correctly safely and have fun. The last day was spent doing a practical and theory. I came top in the practical and the theory. I was chuffed. I had my certificate presented in front of the whole school. It was something Else I had to carry home, when I cycled home.

A couple of weeks later I got a letter from the Cycling Proficiency organisers. I had been selected to go to the County Trials for Cycling Proficiency. It was at the beginning of the summer holidays. It was a lot bigger than I expected. I did not do to badly. I came in the top fifty, out of two hundred and was one of the youngest to compete. I was quite nervous and did my best but I really felt under pressure. My biggest fault was missing a sign to turn right. A marshal was stood in front of the sign as I approached and I did not see the sign until the last second. I only just made the turn but although I did use the right road signals and positioning it was too close to the turning. As usual I went alone, my parents were too busy and I had to cycle to Cowbridge, which was just over three miles away to compete. It was a struggle to cycle home after the competition as I was so tired.

Chapter 30

At the end of the school year, we went to the summer fete at the Hodge Home. My final visit as a member of Maendy County Primary School. There was a bit of a surprise. Gareth Edwards was there to open the fete. As luck would have it, the book club orders had arrived at school that morning. I received my copy of Gareth Edwards' autobiography. I was keeping hold of it until I got back to the house and could put it somewhere safe. Gareth Edwards was such a major personality in Wales, all of us kids were in awe of him. I mustered the courage, pen in one hand, Gareth Edwards autobiography in the other hand, "scuse me Mr Edwards, can you sign my book?" came my request. I'm sure it was as small as I felt, next to a rugby hero. "Mr Edwards" was charm and politeness. He was pleased to talk to me and sign my book. He asked me if I played rugby and what position. I will always admire a true gentleman who was willing to spend time with the public who he performed for so well on the rugby pitch.

That night when I got home, father was cutting up a whole pig on the dining table. He used to think he was a master butcher, but hygiene was not a strong suit. He did buy whole carcasses from time to time as long as they were cheap, really cheap. Half way through cutting up the pig, father commented that there was a lot of blood. He didn't realise for a few seconds it was his blood. He then screamed and screamed, he had chopped the very end of his thumb off about 3 or 4 millimetres. He yelled for a cloth to stop the bleeding. Mother the ever caring wife, bound up his thumb so it looked like something out of a cartoon. Once mother had finished she said "Don't think your disappearing up the hospital leaving that there!" Father quickly cut the rest of the pig into large roasting joints. "You can clean this up and put the meat in the freezer Clive." was the demand before father went out to try and get a lift from one of the neighbours to the hospital. As nobody would give him a lift he had to drive himself. Mother told me I had better clean all the mess up that father had created or else. Every time I said I was finished, mother used to rant that I had not cleaned up and it looked worse than ever. I was still cleaning when father came home four hours later. He had his thumb glued back together a dressing and one of those thumb protectors. I got a slap round the head from him and told to "Go the fuck to bed." I disappeared before he had chance to change his mind.

Father milked it for all it was worth of course. He had a week off work, but still did the driving for the Aubrey Arms when required. I suppose it was easy money for such little work.

Chapter 31

When I went to my Gran's for my annual week at her house in Cardiff, I made sure my bike was locked. Simon had crashed his bike and wreaked it a few weeks earlier and I didn't trust him not to ride my bike, so I padlocked it up, and put a combination bike lock on as well. The week away was quite good. I was able to play with other kids. My cousins were normally around as they didn't live that far away. I caught minnows and sticklebacks in the park at the end of the road. There was another park, Roath Park, which had swings and slides and other playground equipment. Gran always fed us well and it was nice to sleep in a nice bed, hot water for a bath every night and no abuse.

One day I went up to my cousins house in Pentwyn, a suburb of Cardiff. It was a bright sunny day, Gran was cooking and I guess she wanted us out of her hair. I was given instructions on what time to get back to tea and my bus fair. So the day was spent messing around with my cousins, we made a rope swing over a stream.

What really bothered me was when I got back to the house with my cousin Paul. He was a couple of years older than me and much more streetwise. He brought in his ex girlfriend who was about the same age and her younger sister. There was some banter between Paul and this girl, Maria. Then Paul turned round and said "I've shagged her so many times my dick hurt." I was taken aback. I went bright red, I didn't know what to do or say. I was stood in the middle of the room and she was sat on the sofa. Paul said I could shag her if I wanted. I still didn't know where to look or what to do. Maria lifted her skirt and showed she was wearing no knickers. Then Maria leant forward and slid off the sofa and on to her knees and made a grab for the button on my jeans. "Get your cock out for her Clive." was Paul's response. I pulled away from Maria. She said "Don't you want to shag me?" You've seen my fanny, it's only fair I see your cock." I was dumfounded, disgusted shocked. I left the room as quick as I could, Maria followed trying to grab at my trousers. My only escape was to lock myself in the toilet. I could hear Paul laughing. I don't know if he really wanted me to have sex with this girl or was teasing, but it seemed for real. If I had had sex with this girl it appeared that Paul wanted to watch.

Paul appeared some time later. He was on his own. I had stayed in the living room since he had left with the girls. "You'd better not tell mum!" was his demand. I'll smash your face in while you are sleeping if you do." I had no intention of telling my Aunt. What would I tell her! It was confusing, I knew I shouldn't be doing things like that, not at my age. I suppose the biggest thing was that I was really embarrassed. What Paul said made no difference to me as to whether I told or not.

When I came home I found my bike was wreaked. My brother with my father's help had cut both locks off with bolt cutters, so Simon could use my bike while I was away. The front forks were bent so badly that the buckled and crescent shaped front wheel was pressed hard against the frame, the paint was scratched all over the seat was broken as were both mud guards. I went mad I was shouting at my brother and father, until my father's fist hit me in the face and knocked me to the ground. I was dazed, my vision was blurred, just as I was coming to my senses, my father said "Simon, teach him a lesson!" I was still on the floor when Simon's foot connected with my head. I felt several more kicks to the head, before my father said, "Watch his face, hit him in the body!" I took several punches and kicks to my body, it seemed to last quite a while, but I guess it always does, but probably only lasted a couple of minutes. I took the beating, I didn't come to my senses until a little while afterwards.

A couple of days later Mr Fowler asked where my bike was. I told him Simon had crashed it and it was too damaged to ride. At the weekend my father came home with a new front fork and wheel. He told me that I owed him £10 for the parts, which he insisted I pay him. He told me that I would have to fix my bike as I had the parts. I did my best, and the new parts did fit, but my bike was not right and whatever I did I could not make my bike ride straight. I put the bike in the garage, as it could not be ridden properly. My father tried to chastise me for wasting money on the parts, but I stood my ground and explained that even though the parts fitted the frame was not straight and no matter what I tried I could not get my bike to ride safely. A couple of days later I took my bike up to the workshops and said to my father that perhaps he should try and fix my bike as I couldn't. A couple of the fitters came over and asked what the problem was, so I explained the problem with my bike. They had a look and said "OI Chat (My father's nick name) you'd better get your boy a new bike, this one's too far gone to fix!" I sort of felt justified.

Chapter 32

At the start of the autumn term I started Cowbridge Comprehensive School, something that I was glad of at the time. It meant a School uniform, which meant some new clothes. Well it meant one school shirt, one pair of trousers one blazer one winter coat, one pair of socks and pants and proper sports kit. There was a list of clothing that the school was strict on every child having, so it meant new clothes, and as there were only certain clothes shops allowed to sell the school uniform it meant better quality clothes than I had been wearing. It was up to me to keep them clean, and launder them. It was difficult keeping things clean with only one set of clothes. As for shoes, as I was the same size (a UK size 7) I would have a pair of my father's steel toe capped work boots, that my father got free from work. My brother Simon who was in the year above me had a nice new pair of Dr Martins. However, Simon's reputation for being Stig of the dump preceded me. So some of the kids there were less than friendly towards me. Then again compared to my home life, the treatment I received was not so bad. One thing I did enjoy about school was the lunches, this was real good food. The other kids thought I was nuts, but they didn't know what the food was like at home.

I turned up for the first rugby training session. Mr Glan Williams decided that I was an open side flanker. I wasn't happy as I had played hooker at Junior School and I thought that was my only position. Nick Moteshead was chosen to play hooker and team captain, something else that I thought that was wrong. Mr Glan Williams knew something about rugby though, I think I turned out to be a fairly decent open side flanker. The biggest lesson I learned as an open side flanker was to be first to the breakdown, then first to the next one. The other piece of advice that stuck was a good flanker should make a good centre and a good centre should make a good flanker. I suppose as a flanker it meant learning handling skills running with the ball and even kicking the ball. As for the centre, it meant tackling and if making or receiving a tackle, then knowing how to deal with things at the tackle area. I was always given the number six jersey but seven is the position that I played. I learned my craft, and took in all the advice and rules that I could. I was not the tallest but was able to out jump taller boys in the line out just by positioning and timing my jumps better. I was able to put players in an offside position very easily. I also enjoyed tackling the opposition's fly half or putting him under pressure. I enjoyed running round chasing the ball all the game. One move that Mr Glan Williams taught me was from a set piece when we had possession was to loop between the two centres and take the ball on and break the gain line and off load the ball in the tackle to the Centre who by this time should be at full speed. It sort of made me an extra man in the backs and gave us an overlap. The rugby pitch was the one place that I was not picked on or made fun of. There were rules to follow and there was a referee there to make sure that the rules were followed. It meant I could give 100% to the game, and if I put in a good tackle then that was ok, I wouldn't have five or six boys jumping me after the game.

Chapter 33

At school there was one kid in particular who used to pick on me, Michael Gibson. He used to push me around hit me throw my bag about and call me names. It was like water off a ducks back to me. When I did stand up to him, he would summon his accomplices to rough me up. I learned to play the game though and he soon left me alone. I suppose there were more kids to pick on so he was too busy to bother with me. I must admit I did feel rather alone. I would be taunted for my clothes that were bargain basement as were my shoes, my PE kit, even my school bag was a reason to make fun of me. My father's response to such things was for me to walk away, "it takes a bigger man to walk away than to stand and fight." Would be what my father would say. Sometimes though you have to stand up for yourself even if it means you lose the fight. What I found confusing was, most of Gibson's cronies were ok on their own but followed Gibson's lead so easily. I never knew where I stood with these guys, nice one minute, next they would indulge Gibson's latest form of bullying. Gibson always seemed to have a chip on his shoulder, he was smaller than me and ginger so I don't know what caused him to act the way he did. To be honest I don't really care.

I remember I got into an argument with Ian a guy in my year. So a fight was arranged for lunchtime behind the class rooms. Before the fight Gibson and his gang came over to me and warned me that I was not allowed to kick the other guy because of my shoes. I said in that case he's not allowed to kick me either. Gibson told me that if I kicked the other guy him and his gang would start on me there and then, but if the other guy wanted to kick me that was up to him. I said I'd take my shoes off then and wear my plimsolls, Gibson said it didn't matter as I had been warned about kicking. Come the fight it was pretty even. I had a bloodied nose and the other guy had a cut lip. As he couldn't get the better of me he started kicking me and saying "ha ha you can't kick me back can you!" Still things were even. Then a group of boys and girls came round the corner hearing that there was a fight going on. When they found out about the "rules" they broke things up. I had a hand cleaning myself up from a couple of older boys. When I left the boys changing room, a girl from my class came over. We sat down and talked, she told me how unfair she thought the fight was and that it was wrong how Gibson and his gang treated me.

Chapter 34

My brother Simon wanted to join Air Cadets, as he was thirteen. My father was hoping that Simon would be the Windsor Davies of Air Cadets. However, Simon was average at best, even though he thought he was the best cadet in the world. My father had not long done a first aid instructor course at his work so he volunteered to be a first aid instructor for the Air Cadets. I got the impression that he wanted to act like Windsor Davies as if he was an instructor, but he was only ever a civilian instructor and not a Cadet instructor.

It was also decided that I would go to Air Cadets. Although I was too young to officially join the CO a Mr Cartwright said I could attend. I was made to go each week, attend the lessons, aircraft recognition and other subjects. At first the Air Cadets met in a community centre. A couple of years later they had their own building that was paid for by fund raising done by the cadets. I guess there was funding help from somewhere.

In the autumn of my first year at comprehensive, Mr Cartwright was able to get access to a swimming pool in a town called Pontyclun. I was unable to swim but enjoyed going to the swimming pool. We had the pool once a week for a few months. Mr Cartwright took the time to teach me how to swim. Most of the other boys just wanted to mess around, but I wanted to learn how to swim. Some other boys including my brother Simon were given the same opportunity to learn to swim, but they mucked around. I wanted to learn how to swim so I could have proper fun in the pool. I went from not being able to swim to passing my 1500 metres badge in 8 weeks. In another 8 weeks I passed my Gold Silver and Bronze life saving awards, just in time for our access to the pool to come to an end which was a big shame as I was enjoying it so much. Looking on the bright side I was fifty pence better off a week, as I had to pay for myself.

Chapter 35

When riding horses on the competitive side, there was little to touch me. I seemed to win everything I entered. Not because I loved the riding, it's just I was competitive. I enjoyed beating my siblings with ease. They lived and breathed horses but I found it easy to beat them, especially when it came to show jumping. It was just the competition that I enjoyed. As time went on though it wasn't enough. I was turning up late on Saturdays as in autumn and winter I was playing rugby for the school on Saturday mornings, and if it was an away match I would often get back to Cowbridge after twelve o'clock so I got some lunch and went home. I often stopped at Jack's fish and chip shop. Everyone called it greasy Jacks. I had money in my pocket on Saturday so I used to buy lunch. It was bliss to have the house to myself. There were the usual moans about me not going up the stables after rugby, but I always said I got dropped off at home by the bus and it was too late to go up there anyway, or that I didn't have the bus fare to Cowbridge.

As pocket money was non-existent for me I had to find some way of earning some money. As we lived in the middle of nowhere there was not much about. My mother's boss went on holiday and apparently asked my father to look after his car. As usual the car was treated like a dustbin. My father ever the one to show off, invited every kid from our little estate for a ride in the Jaguar. Then by luck I was told to clean my mother's boss's Jaguar XJ6 so it was clean when he go back. When he collected the car he told me I had done a good job and gave £2. He also asked if I could clean his car every week, something which I agreed too. So early every Saturday morning I used to walk the mile to the pub/restaurant where mother worked to clean her boss's car. Then I was taken to the riding stables or dropped off at the school if there was a rugby match.

Chapter 36

When I was twelve I had my first Girl friend, Judith. We went out for quite while I went to her home a few times and met her parents. We eventually finished but we did remain friends for the rest of our school days. That year we came second in the county championship in Rugby. We lost only two games that year both to St Cires in the cup and league both times by a close margin.

I only missed one game in those first two years of senior school. That was due to a large burn on my face that happened when my parents were out. As the coal bill hadn't been paid, the fire hadn't been lit. We had a back boiler to heat the water, so no fire no hot water. We used a Baby Burcco water boiler to heat the water. It was perched on a stool next to the bath. When the water was hot enough I tried to move the Boiler a little closer so that the water went into the bath instead of down the side. That's when the boiler fell over and splashed half my face and arm. The trip switch was tripped and all the lights went out. Simon was the only other person awake and he was panicking, so I had to unplug the Baby Burcco before running down stairs, switch the electricity back on before filling a bowl with cold water so I was able put my face in cold water, this prevented my face from scarring. I was not able to put my arm in the water, then again I barely felt anything from my arm. When my father arrived home he had a friend with him. I was taken to Bridgend hospital. I was examined by Dr Chris Williams, brother of the Welsh rugby player JPR Williams. I was given some burn cream and instructions on how to use it. At school we had a game 6 days later and my face hadn't healed. The team captain Nick Moteshead told me the day before the game I was dropped due to my burn. Moteshead was in Gibson's gang and took delight in telling me the news that I had been dropped. He also made remarks about how a freak like me wouldn't be allowed on the rugby pitch anyway. I assumed he was referring to the burn on my face. The following Monday our PE teacher Mr Glan Williams called me to his office and wanted to know why I didn't turn up. I explained what happened, Mr Williams said he was the only person I have to listen too when it comes to team selection, and that my name was always first on the team sheet. Mr Williams said he would sort out Nick and tell him that he didn't pick the team. When the burn healed, I was very fortunate that I had no scaring on my face. I had a small scar on my left arm that remains today.

Chapter 37

The only time I was really happy as a child was when I was either playing rugby or running. I also found that people treated me differently when I was successful. This treatment only lasted for a short time afterwards but things then returned to normal. Looking back I don't really think I was the sole reason for how I was treated by others, but the family that I was part of. Think of the Beverly Hill Billies in South Wales and you may get some idea of what my family appeared to the outside world.

A turning point was when I was twelve, when I took the bamboo cane off my mother who was trying to hit me with it. I snapped the cane and put it in the fire. Then again the physical pain was not my mother's only controlling weapon, she was a master of manipulation and mind games and turning people against each other.

Mother always liked to be the centre of attention. She had been back and forth to the doctors for months, first this complaint then that complaint. she told everybody she had all sort of things wrong with her. So time came that she was admitted to hospital. We were allowed to visit mother on the night after her "operation". She was telling us all that this and that had been done, a dislodged kidney and a bunch of other stuff, but nothing really made sense. So I went to find someone to talk to. I found a doctor and asked what was going on with my mother as she said there was so much wrong, and I wanted to know what was being done. "I'm sorry son, but your there is nothing wrong with your mum, she was in for a sterilisation." I went back to the ward. "What did the doctor say?" was an inquiry from my siblings. "What's a sterilisation?" I asked mother. "Don't bring that little bastard here again!" was mother's order to my father as she back handed me across the face.

As I was not allowed to go to the hospital the following night my father deposited me and my siblings at my Grandparent's maisonette (Mother's parents). As usual it was shoes off at the door. Once we were fed my grandmother decided we would all have a bath. One by one we were lead into the bath room for a bath while grandmother washed. I was last in. I ran a clean bath and was just getting undressed when my grandmother appeared. "Come on hurry up get in so I can wash you." I was taken aback, there was no way I was having her wash me let alone stay in the bathroom while I got undressed and got in the bath. So once she left I got undressed and into the bath. I was nearly finished when she came rushing in. "Don't forget to wash your bottom." "Get out get out get out!" I shouted, she left but left the door ajar. I quickly finished washing. and jumped out. I slammed the door shut, but there was no lock. So I stood against the door while I dried myself and then got dressed. I didn't talk to my grandmother for the rest of my time at my grandparents place. There were raised voices when my father came to collect us kids. I didn't hear what was said but my grandmother was not happy. That was the last time I went to my grandparents place apart from the annual Christmas pilgrimage. The following day mother came home, telling all who would listen how she had six operations in one. First it was this then that, so many different stories, but as long as she was the centre of attention it didn't matter. Mrs Fowler was one who was not taken in by mothers claims. So I asked her what a sterilisation was. She laughed, "Thank you Clive you have made my day!" she said. Mrs Fowler explained what a sterilisation was to me. Mother still milked it for all it was worth for as long as she could.

Chapter 38

That winter was really bad. Snow covered the country with record snow falls and freezing temperatures. There were reports of Lorry drivers with frozen diesel who were lighting fires under their fuel tanks to try and defrost the diesel. We were snowed in. There was three to four foot of snow but there were drifts up to thirty feet. The snow fell so quickly and the wind was gale force and the wind and snow was relentless. The only way to get food milk or more importantly for my parents cigarettes was to walk the two miles through the snow and across country to the nearest garage. The first time we went father came with me, I guess he didn't trust me with the money. He found it hard going especially on the way back, he wasn't used to that amount of physical exertion. Father collapsed about half a mile from home. I had to drag and carry him and the provisions until we got back to the house. By the time I got back I was exhausted, father wasn't exactly a small man at about fourteen stones. Father didn't make any effort to help me or himself. He was conscious but he just laid there like a lump of dead weight. It was really frustrating, he would not do anything to help, even though he was capable of walking with my support, or holding the provisions while I carried and dragged him. I had no help once inside the house and father had no sympathy from mother. I plonked him in the chair in front of the fire. Mother told me to make her and father hot drinks which I did while I sorted out the provisions.

As father was clearly not up to the task of going to get any food or supplies it was left to me. After all my younger sibling couldn't go they were to young and Simon well you know he was special. so every couple of days for the next three weeks I went to the garage a couple of miles away. As I had to go and feed the horses I went to the garage on the way back. About half way through the three weeks the main road was starting to get some traffic, mainly farmers in their Land Rovers or tractors, and some lorries. I would sometimes get a lift. It worked out well as it meant that I could get warm and being dropped off at Tree Ashes meant I could cut through the workshops. The road was cleared to here first, although there was lots of heavy equipment most of it was frozen solid and wouldn't work. One thing that really puzzled me was father always boasted about having to dig the snow ploughs out during the winter time when he lived in Brecon. This never happened this year, even though there was a lot of heavy equipment. The Caterpillar Bulldozer was huge but I do know that it's blade was to wide to go down our country lane, but there were other diggers and tractors, graders that could have cleared the road down to our estate but they were never used.

Chapter 39

That summer Simon was away on Air Cadets summer camp. Nigel was at Gran's house in Cardiff and Caroline was stopping at a friend's house. We were waiting for Simon to get home from camp, he was due back in Cowbridge about midnight. My father suggested a curry. Mother was in agreement so off I went with father to Rhoose where the Indian take away was that he used. It was probably the cheapest around, but as usual the money he saved on the take away was less than he spent on petrol. My father needed someone to carry the food. When we got there my father placed his order and mother's order they wanted hot curries the hotter the better. I was stood by the window looking at the menu, my father said "What do you want?" I asked my father for a chicken tikka I didn't like the hot curries. When the order came I was surprised how much there was. The bag was huge. So I performed my pack horse duties and carried the food to the car and then from the car into the house. When the food was dished up my father's plate as usual was stacked so high I was sure some was going to fall off. Mother's plate was pretty full too. I had to tell father to stop when there was enough on my plate. There was no way I could eat one of his sized portions of food, although my brothers could. As soon as the food went into my mouth I realised that this was not chicken tikka. I almost chocked. I said I couldn't eat that it was too hot! Mother went nuts, she said I had better eat it after father went all the way to Rhoose to get the curry. My father was sat laughing, he said he ordered me a vindaloo. They both pressurised me to eat the curry with threats, finally mother said if I didn't eat all the curry I would have to give my father the money for the curry as they couldn't afford to waste food. I had eaten about a quarter of the curry I couldn't eat anymore, so I took £2 out of my pocket and threw it at my father and stormed off to bed. When I came down later after father had collected Simon I could hear my parents tell Simon about what happened with the curry, they were all laughing at how I had reacted at how hot the curry was. I thought their time would come. Every time for the next few weeks I was instructed to make a coffee for my parents I would accidentally muck it up. Either too little milk so it was really hot or no sugar to much instant coffee. It wasn't long before the demands for coffee stopped.

Chapter 40

Just after the October half term I was waiting for the School bus. The Fowler boys were there, when my brother Simon came down to where we met the bus at the end of our road. Simon started shouting at me for not waking him up and that he didn't have time for breakfast and that it was all my fault. I told him that I had woke him up but it was not my fault he went back to sleep. He knew I was right but wanted to blame me for him falling back to sleep, he never did take responsibility for anything. Simon threw a punch, it was so easy to dodge. He lunged at me head down, I just grabbed him in a head lock with my left arm. I told him I was not going to fight him, It was what had been drummed into me because of Simon's "condition". Simon was swinging punches No punches really connecting with any force, but he would not stop. Thing was, I was taller broader fitter and stronger than Simon now and I'd had enough I just started punching Simon in the head again and again, all the years of having to accept his bullying ways because I was told by my parents I was not allowed to defend myself, retaliate or stand up for myself against Simon because of his "condition" came to a head. Robert was shouting at me "Go on Clive hit him!" So I did a lot. I had hold of Simon's head in one hand and had plenty of room to swing as hard as I could and connect with Simon's head.

Simon started to crumple. I released his head I thought he had had enough, he half lunged at me, I brought my knee up into his stomach. That felled Simon. "I said I didn't want to fight you! You wouldn't leave it, I'm not your punching bag." Robert just laughed at Simon on the floor. Simon Fowler looked surprised and didn't know what to do or say. Simon was sitting on the floor when the school bus came but Simon went running home instead. Oh well I suppose I'll get it when I get home I thought. I was in late as I had rugby training at school so by the time I got home mother had gone to work. When I got in Caroline said "Mum's not happy with you, and she says you have to make tea for all of us." She was really whiney and patronising. Me cooking tea was the least of my worries, it meant I had something to eat and something that I liked. So I did some boiled potatoes and a few other vegetables and some sliced meat. Simon came in when tea was ready. "I wanted chips!" Simon said. "Tough, if you wanted chips you should have made them," was my response. "You haven't given me enough." I told Simon that there wasn't anymore and if he wanted to be a greedy pig then he would have to cook something else as I wasn't his slave.

The next morning mother collared me before I left the house for school. She wanted to know why I had beaten Simon up. She said "You know what he's like, you should have walked away." I told her I tried and he wouldn't let me. I told her I wasn't going to be Simon's punching bag either. Mother asked why didn't I cook enough food for tea last night. I told her I did and that Simon had more than me and as much as my father. I also said Simon was just being his usual greedy self. She told me to get out and go to school. Simon went into the front room where mother was. I thought I would eaves drop. Mother told Simon that he could no longer use his condition to get me to do what "SHE" wanted and that she would have to figure out some other way to get me to as she wanted. Mother told Simon that I would no longer stand by and let him hit me. Mother told Simon he'd better go to school. She'd written him a note for the previous day. I slipped out of the front door and was at the end of the road when Simon arrived. He stayed the other side of the road from me and was on the bus and sat down before I got to the bus door. I knew that there was trouble brewing for me, but what I had no idea. I just had to do my best to stay out of the way.

Chapter 41

It was about this time that I started to do more away from the house. I joined an athletic club and Air cadets as we lived close to RAF St Athens. I spent time at friends houses, went to Youth Club, anything to get out of the house as much as possible. Although if I needed any sporting equipment like a new pair of rugby boots or running shoes my parents would say that would be my combined birthday and Christmas present and I would not get anything from them or my brother and sister for my birthday or Christmas. I did think that this was wrong, because if my brothers or sister needed anything for their riding, sports equipment for school it was brought for them without question and not referred to as a birthday or Christmas present. They still had their presents at Christmas and birthday.

On the build up to Christmas in Home Economics we were given a recipe for a chocolate Yule log. When I got home that evening from school I told mother what ingredients I needed for the next lesson and told her what we were making. "You'll have to get this lot yourself, I don't have the time or money for your cooking crap!" So at the weekend after rugby I stopped in town and picked up the things I needed. That week in Home Economics I made my Yule log and was really pleased with myself. I got praise from the teacher and an A. When I got home that evening it was like the vultures had descended, I didn't get much of a look in. I did get some though.

A few days later mother came to me all nice as pie, and asked if I could make two Yule logs as she wanted them for Christmas. So that weekend I went into town again and brought the ingredients and I made the Yule logs on the Sunday evening. I covered them with cling film and put them in the pantry. When I came home from school the following day the Yule logs were gone. When I confronted mother she said she had put them away for Christmas. Towards the end of the week mother asked me if I would make some more Yule logs so perhaps we could take them to her mother's at Christmas. I said she had not given me the money for the ingredients for the last lot and that I could not afford to buy any more ingredients. Mother was not happy, she called me a miser and a tight wad. She insisted that I could afford the ingredients if I really wanted, I had my Saturday jobs after all. That Saturday morning before rugby I went as usual to clean Mr Bunn's Jaguar. When I finished he paid me as usual. Mr Bunn asked when would my mother have those other Yule logs ready. I asked what Yule logs. Mr Bunn explained that my mother had made a couple of Yule logs and he brought them off her and was selling them as home made in the restaurant. I was furious. They were the Yule logs I had made and paid for and mother was selling them and keeping the money. I didn't say anything to Mr Bunn, after all it wasn't his fault. I went to rugby but was waiting for mother when she got home after her shift. She asked me if I had brought all I needed to make the Yule logs that she told me to make. I said NO! I told her that I couldn't afford it, and I could not afford to buy ingredients for Yule logs that she was selling and keeping the money. She went off on one as usual, caught bang to rights but as usual I got the blame. She said that she had promised the Yule logs to Mr Bunn and that I had better well make them or else. I dug my heels in and said no and you can't make me. She tried emotional blackmail saying "You don't want me to be humiliated in front of her boss now?" She said she would even pay for the ingredients. I said that she should make them herself, as she is selling them on the basis that she made them. Sent to my room without anything to eat what a surprise.

Chapter 42

The Christmas of 1979 was very memorable. I had got used to the disappointment of Christmas, but my siblings were still excited, I suppose it was a lot better for them as they had a lot more to look forward too I suppose. I was woken up at 5.00 AM by my brother Simon. Caroline and Nigel were already awake playing with the gifts that they had. I just had some coloured pencils and a colouring book cheap and nasty things they were, but that was not unusual for my parents. By 6.00 AM they had convinced me to go down stairs. I did protest that mother and father would not like it but they were so persistent. When we got down stairs, the other 3 immediately piled in and started to unwrap their presents. I only unwrapped one, from my Aunt Angela. It was an Airfix model of a Motor Torpedo boat. I had never made one of these. So I started to assemble the kit, while the other three got on with their presents. About 7.00 AM our parents came down. I was sat cross legged on the floor. I didn't hear my parents come in, as the living room door was open. Then my father's foot stamped on the model I was making. Then came the punch in the back of the head. My mother and father were screaming at me. My siblings turned on me saying that I had instigated coming down stairs and opening presents "Clive made us do it!" was their claim. I got thrown out of the living room and told to go to bed and get out of their sight. My siblings were allowed to stay down stairs. About 10.00 AM I was summoned. "We need coal bringing in!" was my order. When I came back in with the coal my mother said "you ever do anything like that again and you won't have Christmas! You have single handed ruined Christmas for me your father and Simon Nigel and Caroline. What have you got to say for yourself?" "Nothing" was my reply "Well you had better say sorry to everyone." It was easier to say sorry than fight a losing battle, it didn't matter what I said, I was getting them blame, as usual. "You'd better go clean up the mess you made!" was my next instruction. The model was still on the floor where it had been stamped on. It was not repairable, it didn't help that the box had been stamped on, and the parts that I hadn't assembled were all broken. Most of my presents had been opened and just thrown on the floor. I had three Christmas cards, these were from both sets of grandparents and another aunt. All three cards had been opened, the money that was usually inside was nowhere to be seen. I wasn't bothered by the presents, but was furious about the money. Christmas afternoon we were due to go to my mother's parents. When it was time to go my mother said "why aren't you changed?" I said I wasn't going. Mother said that I was. I said tough, I wasn't going until I was given the money back from the Christmas cards. I stood my ground regardless of how much they shouted at me. Eventually after 2 hours of them shouting and me standing my ground the £30 that was in the cards appeared in the front room mantle piece. I hadn't been in the front room for weeks, I hadn't seen anyone go in there all day, but it was made out that I must have put it there. I said I wasn't going until who ever took the money owned up. After half an hour of more shouting mainly at me, Simon came up and said he had taken the money. I don't know if he did or whether he had been put up to saying he'd taken it, but I had an admission. I got washed and changed and off we went. When we got to my mother parents, the usual ritual was shoes off at the door, brand new slippers on, that we had all been given by my mother's parents. They asked why we were so late. Before anyone could say anything I said that it was my fault that we were late and that I wouldn't get changed until whoever stole my money from my Christmas cards owned up. I also said that Simon had owned up to taking the money and that it had been returned. My mother's face was full of thunder. The scowl that she gave me was full of hate. I knew that I would be in for it when I got home. When we got home mother started, but I told her I was only answering her mother's question with the truth.

A few days after Christmas I went into Cowbridge with my Christmas money. I wanted a new watch as the one I had for my seventh birthday had a broken strap for the last year or so, and my parents refused to get me a new strap and told me categorically I was not to get a new strap. I didn't see why but they were quite insistent on it. I had to add some of my own money that I earned to my Christmas money to buy the watch that I wanted. It was a Timex and had dual time, an analogue face with a small digital screen. On the screen you could have the time or date. I chose the date, it also had a chronograph and an alarm. Some people said I was cheating with a digital watch and that was the only way I could tell time. I knew better and responding to these people was a waste of my time.

It was around this time I had my first sexual encounter. I suppose it was clumsy and awkward. The young girl was a bit older than I was and lived not far away from me, and she took the lead. I must admit, it was not any good and I was left feeling disappointed and wondering what all the fuss was about. There is some talk among young boys about having "Done IT" but I couldn't see what all the fuss was about. I never talked about it with the girl or anyone. If I told someone that I had lost my virginity I'm sure I would have been ridiculed and some people would have said I was making it up. Besides I wasn't proud of what I had done, I didn't know if this girl was using me or doing it for a bet, we never spoke about it.

Chapter 43

I gave up the horses as I loved rugby and athletics. It seemed to disappoint some people. My parents were not too happy. As I did well horse riding they seemed to enjoy the status that they gained from me doing well in what is quite a rather well to do past time. Then again that was them all over they liked to mix with the upper class. They liked trying to pass themselves off as in the same social circles as the master of the local hunt and local gentry. When I decided to give up riding, my mother told me not to tell Margret, the owner of the stables. However, at the last ride of the Sunday morning, my mother was standing at the entrance to the tack room. She called me over, and then shouted in front of everyone that I had something to say to Margret and everyone. Margret came over and I told her that it was going to be my last day as I was leaving. My mother piped up, "Did you hear that everyone, he's abandoning you, so you will have to pick up the slack and do his jobs as well as your own!" My mother was not happy. Margret was more relaxed about things, thanked me for all my hard work, and that she was sorry to see me go, but she'd had a inkling for some time that I was losing interest. When I got home, mother said, "As you're going to be home on Sundays, you can cook Sunday lunch! I take it you won't mess that up?"

In the Easter holidays our rugby team were going "on tour." We had a few games planned and were due to stay with our opposite number from the city of St Davids. We had a warm up game against the year above us and trained with them. One guy called Leighton Groves for some reason bit my ear in a ruck. He bit right through, and there was blood everywhere. I had never had an argument with the guy or with any of his friends. I had not even tackled him in the game. To this day I don't know why he did it. Unfortunately it was not seen by the ref so went unpunished.

When we went to West Wales for our tour, there was still a nasty scab on my ear. When we arrived at the school we were introduced to our opposing number, and off we went. I stayed with a boy called Steve and his family. He was a little stand offish to start with. When he was showing me where I was sleeping I asked him if there was something wrong. He asked if my ear was an ear ring piercing gone wrong. Back then male ear piercing was not common and Punk Rockers were the most common group of young males to have it done. I explained that I'd had it bitten in a rugby match against the year above us. Steve seemed relieved and was more sociable after I explained what happened. We stayed up late playing Monopoly and other board games. Steve's family was very nice and made me feel really welcome. We played a couple of games including the St Davids secondary school. We won all our matches and the games were played in a really good manner. I got the impression that those who turned up to watch enjoyed watching a good game almost as much as winning the game. It was such a good atmosphere to play rugby. It was also a good was to finish off a successful rugby season.

Moving into the spring term there was the usual mix of athletics cricket and rounders. I was a member of the school athletics team again. Peter Bridger was an age grade Wales team member. His family full supported him and he had everything he needed for his athletics. I suppose I was his number two at middle distance. I was a member of the 4x400 metres relay as well. Bridger was a member of Gibson's gang, he was very arrogant. It was not unusual for Bridger and myself to finish in the top five. The only training I did outside of school was the run I did at home, no other specific training. Bridger was a member of Cardiff Amateur Athletic Club and it was something he used to brag about.

I also played a little cricket for the school B team. I was a decent bowler and was not afraid to dive to catch a ball, but I was not as good a batsman as I was a bowler and that was probably why I was only good enough for the B team, but I was not a regular.

At the end of the school year, a girl from my school year called Joanne introduced me to her pen friend from Germany at the youth club disco. Her name was Suzi and was the same age as me. Suzi seemed interested in me as a person. Suzi was from a town called Rheinfelden in what was West Germany. Rheinfelden, Mouscron in Belgium and Fecamp in France and Barry in Wales were twin towns and that is how Joanne got to know Suzi. I spent the evening talking with Suzi. When it came time to leave Suzi gave me her address and asked me to write to her. I was not used to a girl being interested in me as a person. From that day I had a pen pal. We would write to each other about once a month. In a way it was refreshing to communicate with someone who was not judgemental.

Our Comprehensive school was split over two locations. The first and second year (now year seven and eight) was the Lower School the upper school was the remainder the other side of town. Next door was the 6th form, but the pupils still wore school uniform and the prefects came from the sixth form as did the head boy and girl. I found in rugby as I was getting bigger and more athletic that I could be a really destructive player. I played open side flanker and was fast and had an ability to tackle which I really enjoyed. I suppose I could take out my frustrations out on the person I was tackling. However, we could not carry through our form from the previous 2 years.

Changing to the upper school we changed PE teachers, a Mr Huw Williams which I did not like at all. Our year's team seemed to be letting the rest of the school down and Mr Williams showed his distaste for our team by repeatedly telling us how rubbish we were. On the rare occasions that Mr Glan Williams took us to our matches and prepared us for the match we did well. By half way through our first term in the upper school Mr Huw Williams passed the coaching selection and all matters relating to our team to Mr Randall a Geography teacher. Some people blamed losing 3 players during the summer as they moved to other schools. Stephano moved to a private school in Cardiff and played at fly half and Chris and Meredith were both the second rows moved further afield. I only ever played against Stephano once after he moved schools. He was a very talented player. Being the open side flanker my job was to tackle him or stifle his play. It was a good contest, which I hope Stephano would agree the honours were even in our personal battle. He was very slippery though.

I asked Mr Huw Williams if I could go to the County trials for rugby. His answer was "You're not big enough strong enough fast enough or hard enough!" I was quite taken aback by his comment. Ironically three weeks later I was getting ready for a match. The opposition fly half came in to our changing room. "Who's the open side?" he asked. "I am." I said "I'm gonna make mince meat out of you today!" and left our changing room laughing. We ran out for the match, I didn't need any inspiration for the game as I always gave 100%. The first time the fly half got the ball, I tackled him hard. The whole game I was harassing him chasing him, he had an awful game as I put him under so much pressure there was not much he could do.

At the end of the game Mr Randall called me over. "Clive these men would like to talk to you." I was asked if I had gone to the county trials. I said no and explained that Mr Huw Williams said I wasn't good enough and told the three men what he said. They were shocked. They explained that they were Welsh age grade selectors and had turned up to see the opposition fly half. They said they were so impressed with how I didn't give him time on the ball, tackled and frustrated him all game. They told me I was their man of the match and that they would recommend to the school that I go to the Welsh trials, even though we lost the match.

Mr Randall was full of praise. He asked if I wanted him to say anything to the team. I said "no" we left it at that. It was my moment of glory, if it had been shared with the team, Gibson or someone else would have said or done something to ruin it.

In this year a girl called Tina Dodsworth joined our year and our form. I really liked Tina, she treated me like a normal person. I thought she was the coolest girl in the school, she was different, a bit of a rebel and totally different to everyone else in school. Tina gave me a record album by the group The Selecter I was in to Ska and Two Tone at the time. I insisted that I give her something for it and made sure I gave her some money. I just thought it was the right thing to do. I suppose I wanted to impress her by making her see that I was decent at heart and not a scrounger. I never saw Tina at the local youth club discos, mind you I doubt if I'd have had the courage to ask her to dance, she was out of my league.

Chapter 44

I liked model making. I used to spend time making aircraft models, my favourite were the World War II planes. I had Spitfires and Hurricanes hanging from fishing line above my bed. I also had a Fokker Wolf and a couple of Messerschmitt fighters being followed by the British fighters. I did have a couple of fighter jets, a Phantom, a Lightening and a Harrier Jump Jet. I had saved up my birthday money along with my Christmas money and put some of the money that I had earned to buy a Lancaster bomber. It was the biggest version of the Lancaster that Airfix did. I spent a couple of months making the Lancaster. I brought all the correct paints and loads of different size brushes so I could put as much detail as possible. Eventually the model was finished. I was really proud, the propellers moved as did the wheels, the undercarriage retracted, the bomb doors opened, the gun turrets moved as did the machine guns. I took the finished model into Air cadets as we were encouraged to show our model aircraft. Everyone was surprised at how much effort I had put in and how well it turned out. Mr Cartwright said I should enter it in the model competition of Cowbridge carnival week. I was very careful when I took it home. I placed it onto of my wardrobe. There was nothing else on top of my wardrobe and I knew it would be safe there. I dusted the model regularly to make sure I kept it in tip top condition. Then one day I came in from playing football as I got home from school, Simon said from the top of the stairs, "Let's see if this can fly!" He threw my model Lancaster down the stairs, it didn't make it half way down the stairs before smashing into the stairs. My mother came out of the living room upon hearing the crash. I was speechless, all that hard work, wasted. Simon said "I only wanted to see if it would fly." I was furious, I said to mother "What are you going to do about it? I spent ages on that model and it cost loads." Mother said "You shouldn't have left it lying around for Simon to get hold of. You know what he is like." "It was on top of my wardrobe, you knew that and so did everyone else." I said. "What do you expect me to do about it?" was mother's response. "Well you can make him pay for it!" I said. "Be serious Clive, he doesn't have any money, so you will either have to fix it yourself or stop moaning." was mother's answer. Once again I knew I had been dumped on. It seemed that I couldn't have anything good, as it would get broken and my parents would do nothing about it. By supporting Simon they seemed to be encouraging him to smash my stuff up. I never made another aircraft model, what was the point, they would only get smashed. I took the rest of my aircraft models in to Air Cadets the next time we met. I gave them to Mr Cartwright. I explained what happened to the Lancaster and said that I didn't want the same thing to happen to the remaining models and I asked him to put them on display or use the jets in particular for Aircraft recognition. The models were put on display in the squadron office. A couple of the jets were displayed at the model competition in Cowbridge week. The Spitfire was highly commended. The name under the models was 293 Squadron Air Training Corps (Cdt Clive Thomas). That was nice of Mr Cartwright.

Chapter 45

My first competition for Barry and Vale Harriers was the Welsh Indoor Championship. I entered the 400 metres and 1500 metres. Bridger was there in his Wales tracksuit. He entered the 800 metres. I won both heats and finals. I wasn't really aware of my achievement. All I knew was that I won a couple of races. It wasn't until years later I found my medals. I had missed the award ceremony and the medals had been given to father. I don't know why father kept hold of them. Bridger didn't win his race.

Later that spring there was the Barry Half Marathon. I was looking forward to it. I had never run that far before. Andrew Ireland the Barry and Vale Harriers coach said I was part of the team and asked if I wanted to run, so I did. 13.2 miles it was quite hard as I was only thirteen. Not long afterwards running such distances for children was banned. However, the race was interesting, there were so many people there running and many more watching and supporting. As the miles went by I started to struggle. The nine mile mark was tough. It was the first time I took water. I picked up after that. I took water at every water station after that. I was more comfortable running after having a drink. The last mile I was flying. I would pick out someone in front of me and try and overtake them. On the final straight about 300 metres long, I passed quite a few people. The final sprint I overtook a man that was being cheered a lot. I crossed the line in front of him. Time: 1 hour 30 minutes and 34 seconds. I shook the hand of the guy in front of me and had a big smile on my face, I was so pleased that I had finished and in a good time. Then I turned round to shake the hand of the guy behind me who was getting all the cheers. It was J.P.R. Williams, the famous rugby player. I put out my hand to shake his, big smile on my face. He just stared at me, glowering at me. He was really upset. "Get away from me boy!" was his only words to me. The press and fans shortly arrived, J.P.R. Williams was all smiles for the press, signing autographs, talking to the press and fans. When the press left he stormed off barging past the fans and spectators, he didn't even stop when he knocked over a spectator and trod on him. Every other competitor stopped to collect their medal and talk to other competitors. Andrew came over to congratulate me. He was really pleased for me. I was really happy. The joy was short lived as my parents turned up. "Clive home now." was my instruction. My father was not happy as he had to travel to Barry to pick me up. I'm surprised he didn't ask me for petrol money. The horses needed sorting. I didn't even have time for a bath, my parents said I would need another bath after seeing to the horses so I wasn't wasting hot water having two baths. So I saw to the horses, went home for a well deserved bath. I was shattered. I had dinner and went to bed. The next morning as usual I had to get up for the horse's morning feed. I was quite sore for the next few days. P.E. was a little subdued for me. The stiffness and muscle soreness passed over the week. It was a good stiffness and soreness, it reminded me of what I had achieved. I didn't tell anyone at school about my half marathon. I didn't think anyone would be interested, or cared. I had no close friends at school, no one I really hung out with. I wasn't a loner, but when I did hang round with other kids, I felt I was tolerated rather than invited. I did join the chess club. I wasn't brilliant but I was ok, not the worst player though. It was a good place to go when the weather was bad. Among the fellow chess club members they invented suicide chess. It was rapid fun way to play chess. If you were in a position to take you had to take the piece. If you didn't take the piece then you missed a turn and your opponent removed the piece that should have been taken. King had to be your last piece, player with no pieces left wins.

Chapter 46

The summer was quite good. I was away a lot that summer. I suppose the only time I was missed was when the horses needed feeding or something else need doing or paying for. I was sent on a school trip to France to see the Normandy Landings, and the Bayer tapestry. I didn't want to go but was told by my parents I was going. It was a long weekend away at the end of the school year. Mind you it was a disaster of a trip. To start the coach was late as it had broken down and a replacement had to be organised. We broke down on the way to Portsmouth twice. It was the first time I had been on a Ferry. I quite enjoyed the crossing to Le Harve. I spent some time on deck. It was so peaceful, especially as the weather was not that good, it was cloudy and cold. I just wrapped up and sat on deck. We were allowed to do what we liked on board, as long as we didn't cause trouble. I spent most of the time alone.

We docked early in the morning. The sun had risen but not by much. It seemed a different world, the weather had changed, it was warm and sunny. The pace of life seemed so much slower. We departed the port and headed for the Bayeux tapestry first. However, on the way to our first destination we had another breakdown. The driver spent ages trying to get the problem fixed.

We eventually got underway. Then on a deserted A road, one of the sky lights came off. We came to an abrupt halt. It was funny seeing this very overweight driver wobble down the road to retrieve the lost sky light. The driver came back read faced huffing and puffing with the sky light in pieces. The drive spent the next half hour patching up the sky light with bin liners. It seemed to last longer that the original sky light.

We made the Bayeux tapestry, it was quite interesting but the site was not as big as I was expecting, and a bit of an anti climax. I brought a couple of souvenirs before we left. We stopped at some sort of hostel that night. We went a saw the Normandy Landings the following day. I found this far more interesting, I looked in the German defences and with the map we had been given tried to imagine how the Allied Forces managed to complete such a major offensive. In a way it was quite moving. Time to go came to soon for me. I could have spent days there.

We boarded the coach and drove to the port without incident. We arrived in plenty of time. We had to wait about ninety minutes until it was time to board. The coach chugged and spluttered onto the ferry. We made our way up to the passenger deck. It was an overnight sailing. I looked round the duty free shops. I had my orders to get some stuff for those at home. I brought some sweets, that would have to do. I then went out on deck again. It was dark, the lights from France looked picturesque. I was wrapped up warm. A girl came over and said hello. She seemed to be quite nice, a bit older than me. He name was Jane and she was on a school trip too, but she was sixteen. Jane was from an all girl's school in the West Country. We spent ages together talking on deck. It was getting cold, so we went inside. There was a large seating area with reclining seats. We went back to where Jane had been sitting before she came on deck. All her school mates were in the nearby seats. Jane leaned over and kissed me. I was quite taken aback, a girl had never shown that kind of interest in me. I was naive and unsure of myself. We kissed for a while, and then her friend who was sleeping on the floor woke up and started kissing Jane. I was a bit confused. Then I felt a little left out. I slipped away, I didn't seem to be noticed. I didn't see Jane on the ferry again. I found a little corner to get some sleep. We docked in Portsmouth, it was a lovely day. The sun was shining. We all got on the bus. It would not start, the bus had to be pushed off the ferry. Luckily the ramp from the ferry was not that steep but the brakes failed on the bus and we crashed into the back of another coach. It was the coach that Jane was on. We all had to get off the bus. Jane's coach was not badly damaged. We were ushered into the arrival lounge. Jane opened the small window on the coach and called me over. She said sorry for last night, she gave me a piece of paper. It had her address on at her school. She asked me to write to her. I was moved on in to the lounge. We waited for hours for another coach to arrive. When it came, the replacement coach was a different company and the coach was really nice. We got back to Cowbridge safely. We learned that the original coach company had gone bankrupt. Parents had been kept advised of what had happened and were there waiting for their children. No one was there to meet me. I slipped out of the school. It took me an hour and fifteen minutes to walk home. "Your back then!" was mother's first words. "So what have you brought me back?" was her demand. I produced the sweets, "That all?" Well I didn't have enough money for anything else. "I Suppose this is for all of us to share! I take you don't want any? There will not be enough for everyone if you do."

Chapter 47

A couple of weeks after the school trip I went away on Air Cadets camp. Air Cadets camp was usually a week away at a RAF base. My first camp was near Bath. Ironically this was to become a familiar place a couple of years later when I joined the Army. Once off the coach it was a mad dash to the accommodation. Nobody wanted to share a room with Simon. I got a room with David Collins. There was another Cadet Squadron from West Wales there as well. They had the far end of the accommodation. There were girls in their Squadron. One particular girl, Adele, was quite friendly towards me. She was quite flirty with me. She did have a boyfriend in her Squadron. They always appeared to be arguing. I offered nothing other than friendship, although I think Adele wanted more. I don't know if this was to make her boyfriend jealous or weather she really liked me in that way. We were shown round some tunnels that were to be used if there was a nuclear war. The tunnels were built as underground weapons storage during World War II. We were also shown a radio station, and were told not to go near the radio antenna as it was a microwave transmitter and this would cook us alive. There was flying and gliding, trips to RAF Kemble, where the Red Arrows were stationed at the time. We spent an hour waiting for them to return from their display. When they arrived back the Red Arrows were booked to give us a tour. On their arrival back at base, they did some manoeuvres before landing. There were only about thirty of us cadets that day, and were spoke to the Red Arrow pilots and even sat in their planes. Before leaving Kemble, we were allowed on a Concord prototype that was still there. Concord did some test flights out of Kemble apparently. The next day was spent orienteering round the local area. My team came second. The weather was great for the whole week, I had little contact with Simon, and I had a great time. I was fed decent food and did interesting stuff. It was a shame to go home.

Over the next few weeks I spent most Sundays competing in Athletics. I was training more often, and was getting better. I really enjoyed middle distance. They were the blue riband events of their era, 800 metres and 1500 metres.

Chapter 48

Back to school in the September, some things changed, some things stayed the same. The daily harassment from Gibson and his cronies still went on, the usual name calling, sometimes my school bag would disappear and I would find it somewhere where I hadn't been that day. They would say that I must have left it there, and that I was so thick that I couldn't remember leaving it there. Things with Gibson would soon enough change.

I was included in a group of boys. Martin Jenkins was the sort of leader of the group, Neil Griffiths and Neil Matthews were also in the group. There were also some girls in the group, Rachel Rees, Jane Fisher and Tina. Martin was popular with the girls. I suppose I was a bit jealous of him. Martin seemed to go out with all the popular girls in turn. I don't know whether there was a conscious decision to include me in the group by an individual or the group. Martin seemed to treat me like his best friend. I suppose it was good to be included I wasn't used to being included.

I was spending more time at Stuart's house. His Mum who I called Mrs H was always so welcoming and friendly. I always felt comfortable and I suppose safe there. Stuart's dad

(Mr H) was a little reserved, but never unpleasant.

Stuart and his sister had to do daily chores and there was rules that they had to follow. They were quite religious but never rammed religion down my throat. There was respect for each other and genuine love. It was a nice place to be, a kind of home I wished I had. Mr H worked at the Ford factory in Bridgend but was always around when needed. Mrs H a lovely lady who enjoyed life, she quite often had a big beaming smile that made me smile. Mrs H was not stuffy or staid as you would think someone so religious is, in my opinion she is how most religious people should be like, warm friendly and with a sense of humour. There was always a cup of tea there for me, although sometimes Stuart liked to rush me. Stuart could not sit still for five minutes at times. Stuart's sister Laurie was a typical young girl, a couple of years younger than Stuart. My sister was friends with Laurie.

Stuart joined Air cadets and Barry and Vale Harriers and was quite a good sprinter but suffered quite a nasty injury to the back of his knee cap.

Chapter 49

I am bothered by one particular rainy October night when I was fourteen. It was the first training session of the month. Although I have very little memory of the night. I remember coming home from rugby training, my mother was at "work" and my father was out supposedly driving the minibus for the employees where my mother worked. My brother Simon was home, Caroline was in her room as was Nigel. I had a bath and sorted myself something to eat. The last thing I remember was talking my dinner plate out and washing it up. I went back into the front room to watch TV and have a cup of tea. The next thing I remember was the following morning being woken up by my alarm, my head was fuzzy I felt confused, I didn't know how I got to bed. I still had my socks on, and my t shirt, something I never did. There was a little blood on my bed and my back side was sore. I muddled through feeding the horses and going to school. I suppose the best description on how I felt was hung over, but very fuzzy. I had nothing to drink, at that time I hated alcohol. It was all very confusing. School was a bit of a blur, I don't think I took anything in. I had a feeling of being dirty, I was confused angry, but not 100% sure why. When I got home from school, I was a bit more with it. When Simon came in, he said "How's your arse?" I was so mad, "How the hell do you know?" Simon just smiled, I went to the kitchen and grabbed a knife, and lunged at Simon with the knife, "What the fuck have you done to me?" I shouted. My mother grabbed me and screamed at Simon to get out. It was all she could do to hold me back from going after Simon. I screamed at her "If Simon's done something to me I'll kill him!" She asked me what happened. I told her what I could remember. She told me that as I had been training that evening I was probably exhausted and as for the blood and soreness that was probably down to piles, as rugby is a winter sport and the cold had probably caused the piles. I wasn't convinced, but I was going to let it go, for now. Mother also said that if I did tell anyone like the police it would be my word against his and she would have to tell the police about my piles, and they wouldn't believe me. Mother told me that the police would ridicule and humiliate me and she asked if I was prepared for everyone to know what happened. Then she spoke as if she was trying to sooth and calm me down, trying to rationalize with me, asking me if I was sure what happened and that it was ok if I had made a mistake. I just found it condescending. I warned my mother though, that if I found out for sure, that Simon had interfered with me I would kill him and that I wouldn't need to call the police! It was a threat I never carried out, but a threat my mother knew I would carry out if anything else like that happened to me. I know that Simon will get his just deserts, in this life or the next.

I had the feeling of being dirty unclean. I did my best to keep myself respectable but this was different. It didn't matter how long I scrubbed myself in the bath or the showers after rugby or P.E. I could not get the feeling of being dirty off me, I tried soap shower gel even bleach at one stage, but nothing could shake the feeling of being dirty. I was very wary when in the bath at home, not only did I lock the door I put a wedge under the door just to make sure no one could come in. I made sure I dressed undressed and changed in privacy. I used the wedge under the bedroom door when I was changing as I shared a bedroom with Simon and Nigel, and at night I got undressed under my quilt. and I made sure Simon was asleep before I went to sleep. I put a pen knife under my pillow just in case. If Simon got aggressive or abusive I would either stare at him or tell him to shut up or else. I'd tell him I wasn't taking any of his rubbish and if he wanted to start anything I would finish it. I would be as assertive in front of my parents, and I made it plain that I didn't care what they said or did, if Simon tried anything with me, I wouldn't stand for it and Simon would get hurt and hurt bad.

Things changed for me from that day, it wasn't just the straw that broke the camel's back, it was more than that, but it had been a long time brewing. I was angry and moody a lot of the time. Nothing in particular seemed to set me off. Mother used to say I had a face like thunder, but I needed to snap out of it or she would knock it out of me. I started listening more to Punk Rock, Stiff Little Fingers, the Sex Pistols, Dead Kennedys, The Undertones and even Crass. I could identify with the anger and hate in some of the songs. The first time I listened to "At The Edge" by Stiff Little Fingers I knew that was my life, but what could I do to change it? Nothing while I was living in that hovel. I knew that I wanted to get out and once I left I was not going to be living back there again. I wasn't going to be picked on any more either by anyone. I didn't care what happened and I didn't care about the consequences, no one was going to push me around anymore.

I must admit, the thought of what I suspect happened really troubled me. I know I wasn't the best student, and that if I had put in some effort I could have achieved much more academically, but school was a real struggle for me, then again so was life in general. It was like I was going through the motions of life. I was so frustrated, this on one occasion I was in class. Things came to a head, some silly disagreement. I was toying with a desk with a metal ruler attached. It had been worked on and I knocked the desk over. The teacher started to tell us off and order was restored. I put the desk back but a small piece of the metal ruler had broken off about two inches long. I picked it up and was playing with it under my desk. It was sharp I stared at it. There seemed to be nothing happening around me, I was focussed on the metal. The next thing I remember I was bleeding from my right forearm. The cut was not that deep but about an inch long and going up my forearm at a slight diagonal. I didn't feel any pain, but it felt oh so good. I closed my eyes and enjoyed the pain. When I opened my eyes, I sort of snapped out of it and put my other hand over the cut and applied pressure. I felt I had to hide it from everyone, it was like part of this secret. I had a wrist band in my school bag, so I reached down and got it out of my bag and slipped it on my right arm and slid it up to cover the cut and put pressure on it. The bleeding stopped by the time the lesson finished. I put my blazer on, it covered up my cut. When I got home, I put a dressing on my arm. I had to wash my shirt by hand as at the time we had no washing machine to get the blood out. I had to dry my shirt for school the following day, as I still only had one school shirt.

Then a few days later I was playing rugby. I was always a good tackler and that was a major part of my game. I just got everything right, I tackled like a Samoan and real big thump and the recipient of the tackle went down like a sack of spuds. It was so satisfying. Perhaps I was taking out my frustrations and troubles out on the rugby pitch. I made another couple of hard tackles in the game, and when I came off the pitch, I felt better than I had for a long time. I was given praise for my "performance." We still lost the game, but I knew I played well.

I started to feel better about myself, when I played rugby, I suppose it was my outlet. I put everything into every game. Although the team didn't win any more games, I was playing better than ever. I was exhausted after every game though, really drained. I never let myself be in the same position as I had been before on that night when I got home. I was careful about what I eat and drunk when I came home from rugby or Athletics club. I didn't trust anybody in the house, I felt even more alone, isolated. I couldn't talk to anyone about what might have happened, who would believe me? I was still confused, moody, upset and I felt degraded, ashamed.

I had a bit of trouble at school. Mr Huw Williams my P.E. Teacher in the upper school and I never got on. We had several fallings out. One day we had a big argument and it very nearly came to blows, I just blew up at Mr Williams I stormed at him after a P.E. lesson fists clenched. I couldn't believe that another boy had been selected instead of me for Cross Country. I had never lost to this particular boy, he was alright, a bit quiet and very intelligent. I always felt that Mr Williams had it in for me, he always seemed to be holding me back. If I wanted to go to the county trials for any sport, he would tell me I wasn't good enough and he wouldn't support me in my ambitions. I knew I was good enough, I was better than the guys who were going to the county trials. I had to go as a guest.

P.E. wasn't the only place where I would lose my temper. I was generally angry, I suppose quite volatile. There was an incident at school. I was called in and asked what I knew about something that had happened that lunchtime. I hadn't a clue, I still don't know what happened. I was walking to class when Martin stormed up to me, he swung a punch. The punch grazed the side of my face. "What the hell was that for?" I demanded. "You grassed me up!" "I don't know what happened at lunch I don't want to know and that's what I told the deputy head!" was my reply. "I'll let you have that one, but you try that again, and I don't care what you do, I'll have you one way or another!" I stood there staring at Martin, he walked off. I picked up my bag and went to class. A couple of days later, Martin came up to me. He apologized. I was surprised by this. He tried to explain that it was his sugar levels being low and he was on the verge of a hypo which was why he swung at me. I was still smarting at the whole incident. I was a little distant not just with Martin but the group for a few weeks. Martin was bending over backwards to be nice to me, trying even harder to include me in everything the group did. I eventually came round, I suppose I didn't have that many friends. Tina sensed that something had happened between us, and she asked me what happened. I told her, she was quite angry with Martin. Tina said she would put Martin in his place.

I also had a bit of a run in with the Deputy Headmaster, Mr Murphy. A boy in my class called Matthew and I were mucking around outside class and we got sent to Mr Murphy. It started by Matthew trying to goat me in to mucking around. Perhaps he was trying to lift my spirits as I wasn't much fun those days. It was the "come on putt them up, the little cuff round the head type of stuff. In the then I started to play. Matthew jumped in a puddle and splashed mud all up my uniform just as the teacher came round the corner. So off we went to Mr Murphy's office.

Matthew got called in first. He was in for what seemed like ages. When he came out he looked rather sheepish. and a bit red faced. He told me to go in and went off to class. Mr Murphy started shouting at me about my appearance and behaviour. Then he said something that really annoyed me. "Simon I've had complaints from some of the teachers about your Body Odour." My mind was racing did he really call me Simon? "Simon you need to smarten yourself up and clean yourself up. While you are wearing that school uniform you represent the school and we can't have you going round stinking up the place!" He went on but I really didn't listen to much I was being told off by Mr Murphy the most scary teacher in the school for something Simon has done. My mind was racing all I could hear was Simon this, Simon that, none of it good. All of a sudden I erupted "SHUT UP!" I caught Mr Murphy mid sentence. Mr Murphy looked surprised and angry and was about to erupt when I said "I'm CLIVE THOMAS not Simon Thomas. Simon is my stinking brother who I wish I would just drop dead. I hate him he is scum! I know he smells I have to live with him. Just don't ever mix me up with him, ever!" I was really forceful, I don't think Mr Murphy was used to being spoken to like that especially by a pupil. His embarrassment was clear. "C C Clive I'm sorry I I didn't realise it was you and not your brother." I'd never seen Mr Murphy like that. I just turned around and stormed out of his office and went back to my class. Afterwards Matthew came up to me and asked what happened, I just said I got told off for the mud on my uniform.

At the end of school I didn't go home on the school bus. I walked in to Cowbridge and found myself in one of the small parks that ran near the river. I was sat on a bench lost in my troubles. I policeman came walking past. I didn't notice him until he said "You alright son?" "Not really" was my answer. "Is there anything I can help with?"

he enquired "Dunno" was my reply. "Come on son you can tell me." So I told him about that night. He looked shocked, I was trying to fight back the tears. Saying it out load to a policeman made it seem so sordid, graphic, painful. He asked if I was sure about what had happened, and I told him no and that was part of the problem. I told him what mother had said, and that she would insist that I couldn't remember because of exhaustion and that the pain blood and soreness was down to piles. I also told him that mother told me it was my word against Simon's and hers. He told me not to worry he would look into things. He asked if he could take me home. I said I wanted to sit by the river a while, the babbling sound of the water was quite soothing.

That night when I got home, I washed and dried my uniform, I suppose to prove to everyone that I was different from my brother. A scrubbing session in the bath was also called for. It wasn't just what Mr Murphy said, I still felt dirty.

A couple of days later the policeman came to see me. He waited until after rugby training and caught up with me on the way to the bus stop. He asked if we could talk. He told me he had been to see mother and questioned her. He told me legally there was not a lot he could do as there was no evidence and that mother was right it was my word against Simon's and her. He said he had threatened her with all sorts but she stuck to her story. He told me that he had told her if anything else happened to me that he would arrest those involved and he wouldn't keep it quiet. He told me that if anytime I needed to talk he would be there.

That night when I got home, there was an atmosphere. Mother was at work, father said "What the fuck have you done to upset your mother now?" "I dunno" was my reply. The next few days, mother just stared at me. Simon stayed away from me.

The next time mother talked to me was when we had to go into Cardiff. We all went. To start with I had no idea as to why we were all going in to Cardiff. Then we got to a mens out fitters. Simon and Nigel were measured up and shown to a rack of suits. They spent ages choosing their suits, trying different suits on standing in front of mirrors. They got new shoes to go with their new suits. When they had eventually finished I was shown to another part of the shop and told to choose a suit off a rail that had a Sale and Seconds sign. I looked carefully, there was nothing that I liked and I said so. "I'm not wearing any of those I don't like them." Mother took me to one side, "Look you little bastard to made enough trouble to last a life time, now choose a fucking suit to go to your Uncle Paul's wedding!" while walking back to the sale and seconds rail, I saw a three piece suit. "I like that one!" It was grey with a blue pinstripe. "It's a little more affordable than the other two suits, shall we try it on?" The salesman said. He measured me and I tried the suit on. It felt nice to have a well made suit on, so much better than anything else I had ever worn.

The salesman added up and I thought my parents were going to cry parting with all that money in one go and not a penny on themselves. I was given all the bags. I couldn't be bothered to argue. We went to another clothes shop but for women this time. My sister took her time picking out the dress she wanted. When mother paid she tried to pass me the bag with the dress in, I just shrugged and said my hands were full. I just got a scowl. We headed back to the car "Am I getting new shoes like everybody else?" "Not after the fuss you made getting your suit. If you would have had one of the cheaper suits perhaps you could have had new shoes." Said mother. "Simon and Nigel's suits cost more than mine and they still got shoes." "You shouldn't have made such a fuss then!" I knew that I was not going to get anywhere, so just walked back to the car. I put the bags in the boot of the car but I put my bag to one side. When we got home I got out of the car and just grabbed my suit bag and went up stairs and hung my suit up in my wardrobe. A few minutes later I was shouted for. "Where are the new clothes?" "I've hung mine up in my wardrobe." Where's the rest?" mother shouted. "I dunno where they left them I suppose." "You'd better go and get them." Was mother's demand, "If they want then they know where they are." I walked out of the room and up to my room.

When the wedding came I kept a low profile. I spent most of the time by myself. I felt as if I didn't belong and nobody seemed to care that I wasn't involved. I didn't eat anything and only had one lemonade. I felt so alone, but then again if I was alone then nobody was giving me a hard time.

Chapter 50

I passed my exam which meant I could get promoted in Air Cadets. My brother Simon had failed his several times. Automatic promotion was not guaranteed though. It was not long before I did get promoted to Cadet Corporal. I also passed my cadet marksman and my RAF marksman. I also started an O Level in Weather and Air Navigation, which was more interesting than it appeared. I started my Duke of Edinburgh award. This seemed to irk my father and Simon, but there was nothing they could do about it. Simon being the eldest was "The Chosen ONE!" My father seemed to think he was some kind of Windsor Davis and Simon was his prodigy. Simon had to do as I said, in Cadets at least, although I did not pick on Simon, I just took satisfaction that I was better than him and the stripes on my arm proved it. I got more assertive with Simon. I made it known to the whole family that I would not take any more shit from Simon. If I had to wake up Simon in the morning the he would get a kick or two or a cup of water thrown over him. If Simon didn't like it, tough he was going to get smacked down literally. Simon now knew I would not back down, and if he pushed it, he was going to get hurt big time! My mother and father knew it too. The poor Simon, "he is not all there" routine was not going to work anymore.

They knew that I would not hold back because of his "condition" as I had in the past.

In the summer I was really struggling with fitness and form in athletics. My times we still ok but had not improved as I and my team coach had expected. I was feeling really run down. A lot of people were saying how pale I looked. Mr Randall a teacher at school and our year's rugby coach suggested I go and see my doctor. I hadn't seen Mr Randall for a couple of months due to the rugby season finishing. Mr Randal said I looked pale and gaunt. I said that I had been feeling run down, lacking in energy.

My mother was against me going to the doctor, she tried her best to persuade me not to go. In the end I told I wouldn't bother. I did go though. I didn't see the "family" doctor Dr Neighsmith. I saw a new doctor Dr Jones, quite a young guy, by far the youngest doctor in the practice. Dr Jones gave me a thorough examination and did some blood tests and a heamoglobulin test. Dr Jones told me that I had an iron deficiency and wanted me to come back in a week. When I did go back Dr Jones said that my iron deficiency was down to diet and that he was concerned about my health and that if my diet and weight wasn't sorted out then he would have to involve other agencies. We discussed what I should be eating, and what I had been eating and why. The only way that this could be resolved is to sort it out myself. It meant me buying some food myself, and choosing the healthy option which wasn't a problem from the menu at the school canteen, it did mean using some of the money from my part time jobs to pay for the meals as my parents would only give me enough for a portion of chips. The other kids thought I was strange for selecting the vegetables and lean meats, instead if chips and other fast food. I wasn't long before I was feeling better though. My skin colour was still pale and some people still commented on it. It did take a few months before my fitness returned, and by that time the rugby season had started, so putting on weight was a benefit. My brother Simon got more money for his school lunch. He had lost quite a bit of weight and mother was worried he was not eating enough. What mother didn't know was Simon was spending his lunch money on cigarettes. The more weight Simon lost, the more money mother gave him. I guess in the end he was getting enough money to pay for twenty cigarettes and his lunch every day, as he started to put weight back on.

The last week of the summer term I also had a problem with my left knee, it was a little sore after competition. I spoke to Andrew Ireland about it and he said I should see my doctor or better still see the physiotherapist that the club recommended. My mother said it was just growing pains and I should not go and going to the doctor was a waste of time. A few days later while walking home from the bus stop my knee locked. I couldn't straighten it at all no matter how hard I tried. When I got in I told mother that I would have to see the doctor because my knee had locked. Mother told me not to be stupid. When my father came in she told me to come in the front room. She told me to sit down. As soon as I sat down my father sort of bear hugged me and held me down. Mother grabbed hold of my leg and raised it and put a stool under it, she put her weight on my knee and bounced up and down until it straightened. This was excruciating and there was a load crack as my knee straightened. I eventually wrestled my father off me. I shouted and screamed at my parents. Mother told me that I was not too big to be put over my father's knee and that there was no need to see the doctor now. I told my mother that I'd like to see my father try and put me over his knee. I hobbled off to my bedroom, my knee was so painful. The next time I was at athletics training I took Andrew Ireland to one side and explained what happened. He was not amused. Andrew gave me some upper body exercises to do and some quadriceps exercises, and told me to rest raise my leg and ice my knee. Andrew said that he would be having words with my father when he came to pick me up. Andrew went ballistic at my father and told him that if he didn't take me to physiotherapist that he recommended then he would be calling the police and reporting my father for child abuse. I have never seen Andrew Ireland so mad.

So after a phone call to Ron Durham the Physiotherapist I had an appointment. So off we went to Cardiff to see Ron Durham. At first he examined me and my parents made sure they gave him the answers. So after a while Ron Durham examined me he put me on a diapulse machine. He told my parents that I would be a while on the machine so they should go and have a cuppa in the cafe down the road and that I would join them when finished. A few minutes after my parents left the machine started to bleep. Ron Durham came in and switched it off. He explained that it helped reduce the swelling. Ron Durham asked me what really happened, and that Andrew Ireland had filled him in. He examined me extensively. His diagnosis was a pulled ligament and fluid had filled the space that the ligament should occupy and was preventing the ligament returning to it's rightful place. He gave me exercises and another appointment. He charged my parents £25 per session and would only accept cash, but he explained that he had over charged my parents so that it would cover the cost of more sessions, as he said that my parents had told him they would only pay for a couple of sessions. My parents were furious of course having to fork out that kind of money and take me into Cardiff and they would have to take me back again. Mother also said that I would have to pay towards some of the cost and that if I told anyone then they wouldn't take me again. So they wanted £10 per session, which I paid. I had five sessions with Ron Durham in all, I don't know if the £50 in total that my parents paid covered the cost, I tried to pay more but Ron Durham would not accept any money from me. The remaining sessions I had to get a bus into Cardiff but that wasn't really a problem. I explained that I had to do hydrotherapy and the nearest pool was Cardiff. It wasn't a million miles from the truth as that was one of the things that Ron Durham had recommended.

I had missed the four days of the last week of school due to going to see Ron Durham and going to the swimming pool, the swimming pool really helped with my rehab, besides it meant a hot shower afterwards. On the last day of school there was the Radio 1 road show in Barry. Mother was going with her friend Pauline. Simon was also going. I said that I didn't see why Simon should go when everyone else has to go to school. Mother said that if I shut my mouth then I could go. I made sure mother wrote a letter to the school and signed it so that I could hand it in when I got back to school in September.

As soon as the bus arrived in Barry I left mother and Simon to their own devices. It was obvious that they were not going to the Radio 1 Road Show, so I went by myself which was fine by me. Paul Young was one of the star guests as was

Howard Jones. they both performed a couple of songs each. I had a great time. I bumped in to Scott Combes another boy in my year at school. Scott was alright and I got on with him quite well. He went to Air Cadets as well so we hung out for the rest of the day. I made my own way home as I had no idea of where mother or Simon were. They got home about two hours after me at about six o'clock. Mother was furious that she would be late for work. Of course it was my fault as I hadn't found mother and told her that it was time to go home because of work. How was I supposed to know where she went, she disappeared. I had no idea where mother went and I wasn't interested either.

Chapter 51

I was fairly successful at the athletics competing in the Glamorgan Young Athletes league then we gained promoting to the British Young Athlete's league, for Barry and Vale Harriers. However, I was serving 2 masters as I was also passionate about my rugby, perhaps this impeded my athletics. Many people said I was not exactly built for middle distance running as I was too muscular and most middle distance runners of the time were slim. But I was competitive from 400 metres up to 3000 metres and cross country. I suppose I was confused about my commitment to either sport as I was generally confused about life in general.

1982 was quite a memorable year. The Falkland Islands had been invaded by Argentina and Margaret Thatcher had order a Task Force to the South Atlantic to retake to Falkland Islands. I was glued to the news every night, following what happened in the conflict. First South Georgia was retaken followed by an assault on the main Falkland Islands. Several ships were destroyed by the Argentines using French made Exocet missiles. This was infuriating. I thought the French were supposed to be our allies, and in the Falklands French made missiles were destroy our ships and killing our men. The French claimed that the missiles were sold by third party countries such as Israel. After weeks of fighting the Falklands Islands were returned to British rule. The people of the Falkland Islands fully supported being under British rule and being part of the United Kingdom.

After the fighting had stopped, I watched a film of how the Argentine prisoners were handled, and repatriated. I was amazed at how well they were treated by our Armed Forces. After all only a few days ago these Argies were trying to kill our Armed Forces and here they were being fed and given shelter and treated with respect. There were celebrations when the Task Force returned triumphant from the Falkland Islands. A permanent Garrison was established on the Falkland Islands, to protect against any further invasions of our interests in the South Atlantic. I knew what I wanted to do with my life after school. I wanted to join the Armed Forces. I guess a natural for me would have been to join the RAF as I was in Air Cadets. I did make initial contact and application to the RAF. Obviously as I was too young I was told to come back when I was sixteen to start the application process in full.

One Sunday father was taking me to Air Cadets, as there was flying on. As it coincided with father taking lunch to my siblings at the stable he couldn't really avoid giving me a lift especially as he was a civilian instructor. So we started up the back lane past the garages. A car was coming the other way at high speed. Father pulled in front of the garages, but the car skidded and came into the side of us. The impact knocked the wind out of me, and my neck was sore. The driver of the other car was Steven Jones who lived in the bottom houses next door to Stuart. He backed his car up and got out to assess the damage. The damage to father's car was not bad the front wind and door were dented, but he was able to open his door. Steven was very apologetic. He insisted that he would pop up to our house later to sort this out as it was obviously his fault. I got dropped off just in time. It was a good day out and I learnt a few new things flying.

When I got home mother and father were there. I put some soup on while I washed and got changed and was on my way down stairs when there was a knock at the door. It was Steven, he had David Matthews and Neil Beams with him. I called father. When he came Steven said he was not going to pay for the damage, and father could do what he liked as he was not getting anything out of him. Father erupted with rage and told Steven to "Fuck Off out of it and he would sort him out." Father never showed his anger at anyone apart from me. Father slammed the front door and stared at me. I said "Well your insurance will be able to sort it out." "You fucking little bastard, this is all your fault, if I didn't have to drop you off in Cowbridge, this would never have happened.!" By this time mother had come out and had obviously heard what had happened. "Typical of you to fuck things up. I've a good mind to make you pay for the damage!" shouted mother. Mother turned sharply and went back in to the front room while father stared at me. I wasn't going to take this, it wasn't my fault that Steven was driving like a maniac. I couldn't understand why father just didn't contact his insurance, they would sort it out, surely? "You were going to Cowbridge anyway, you would have been there even if I wasn't in the car!" I could see father getting really angry "I've a good mind to give you a good hiding!" ranted father. "Go on try it, I don't care!" I squared up to father, I was slightly taller than him and broader across the shoulders. I stood eye to eye with him. He pushed me out of the way and stormed in to the front room. Relieved I let out a sigh and went in to the front room. I past father puffing on a cigarette on my way to the kitchen. The soup was gone. "Where's my tea gone?" I demanded. "If you think you're eating here you can fuck off and forget it." said mother. I looked in the bin, she had thrown even the saucepan in the bin.

I went upstairs, and got some money from my hiding place. As I came down stairs mother shouted "You owe me a new saucepan." I left her to it as I shut the front door. I walked to Bonvilston a village two miles away. There was a garage with a shop. I brought a pie and some apples, a can of lemonade and a chocolate bar. I walked the long way home through the lanes. I knew father would not come this way as it was too far out of his way. By the time I got home, there was no one home, the house was dark. I sorted my stuff out for the following morning and went to bed. About eleven o'clock everyone came in. I could hear the noise of talking and the TV downstairs. When Simon and Nigel came in to the room, the light went on. "How was your fish and chips Nigel?" Simon obviously said for my benefit. "Lovely, worth going in to Cardiff for." I didn't stir, I pretended to be asleep. Simon and Nigel made quite a bit of noise until they decided they wanted to go to sleep. They had an argument about who should turn the light out. They even suggested waking me to get me to turn the light out. Eventually Nigel turned the light out. I reached under my pillow and clasped the knife that I had put there. I eventually fell asleep with the knife tightly in my hand.

Chapter 52

I also got involved with a guy called Steve. He was a lot older than me at nineteen. I was encouraged to get involved with Steve by my parents. Steve had been in trouble with the police and had a younger sister Tracey in the sixth Form at school. Steve had spent time in borstal and enjoyed a bad boy reputation. Not long after Steve and I became acquainted he got kicked out by his parents. My parents were only too quick to give Steve a place to stay, even if it was on our sofa. While staying with us Steve commented that I should be doing more round the house to help my mother out. I told him I had spent years running round after everyone trying to keep the place tidy only for the rest of the family to treat it like a dustbin. I told him that I did more than my fair share round the house and washed my own clothes paid for my own milk and some of my food, as well as paying for my hobbies that my siblings had paid for by my parents. The longer Steve stayed the longer he got to see that I was telling the truth.

One day Steve said he had to go into Cardiff. My mother asked if he could take me. Mother told me I had to cash her Child Benefit, something I had done many times. So off we went on the bus to Cardiff. Steve got off in Bonvilston, where his parents lived. He beckoned me to get off. He said he had something he needed to collect from his house and that he was going now as he knew his parents were out and he didn't want another row. When we got to the house, Steve went straight for the garage, he unlocked and opened it. Once inside he got his 125cc motor bike. He called for me to grab the two helmets that were on the shelf. He ran off pushing the bike. I caught him up carrying the helmets. "What are you doing?" "I need my bike." Once round the corner he started up the bike, grabbed his helmet and told me to get on and put the other helmet on. I got on and we went to Cardiff. I went swimming and did some clothes shopping. When it was time to go, I made my way to the Post Office. I collected mother's Child Benefit. I put the money inside the Child Benefit book and folded it and put it in my back pocket. My pockets were not that secure and I was constantly checking. When we got back to the bike I took out the Child Benefit book. The money was gone. I couldn't believe it, I had the book but the money inside was gone. I couldn't understand how this happened. I retraced my steps, back to the Post Office. I asked the Post Office staff if I had left the money there or if it had been handed in. I was at a loss as to how the money had gone missing. The only time the book and money were out of my hands was when I handed it to Steve to hold while I took my news paper out of my back pocket and put it inside my jacket (It had no pockets but it was short and had an elasticated waist) then I got the book back from Steve and put it in my back pocket.

Of course mother was furious with me and told me I had to repay that money. She told me that the money I lost was supposed to be for me to go to France for my Athletics club for the annual twin town sport festival next summer. I felt that this was used just to rub it in that I had lost the money.

Later that day I saw Steve and mother very cosy in the kitchen. Steve handed mother some folded money. Mother gently touched Steve's face with her hand and smiled at Steve. Mother kissed Steve gently on the cheek, they both almost jumped out of their skin when they realised I was there. Ironically during that day I had to pay for everything as Steve said he had no money. When I questioned mother later about the money Steve gave her she told me that it was for Steve's keep while he was staying there. I told her that he had no money and she replied that it was what he had put away and would not touch it as it was for his keep. I didn't believe her but was getting more suspicious of Steve.

That evening I went with Steve to put his bike back at his parents. His father heard the garage door open and came out. He was furious with Steve. He told Steve unless he could mend his ways he would not be welcome back home.

Steve's dad said that he did not blame me as he knew Steve had led me astray. Steve's dad took the bike and told Steve that this would be the last time he would be using his bike, as it would be sold to pay for his court fines, and in the mean time he was moving it to somewhere safe.

When Steve and I got back to my house he was a bit mad. Mother asked what happened and Steve said I had made so much noise putting the bike back, it had alerted his father and it all kicked off from there. Mother commented that it was typical of me to mess things up.

A week later Steve came home from his community service job at an old people's home quite excited. He said he had been given permission to use the van from work for a night out and showed me the keys for the van. Steve asked if I was up for going into town. I said yes there must be a film on. So once it was dark off we went to the old people's home where Steve was doing his community service. I did not realise the significance of it being dark. As we approached the home, Steve ducked down and told me to do the same. We crept up to the van (It was a grey Mini Van), Steve fiddled with the lock and got the door open. Once inside he made sure the van was in neutral and released the handbrake. Steve told me to push the van out of it's parking space. His voice was whisper quiet and if I made to much noise he quickly shushed me. He came up to me and said we had to push the van out and keep the noise down as we couldn't disturb the residents. A man in his 60s came out. "what's going on here?" he shouted in an angry voice. Steve shouted "Run!" I was gone, the old man went after Steve, he was slower and although tall at about 6'2" was very slim. I was gone like a rocket. The old man didn't catch Steve. We met up about ten minutes later, the other side of town. I was furious. I shouted at Steve, "What the hell was that all about? You said you had permission to take the van! You almost got me to help you steal that van!" I then punched Steve right in the mouth. He never expected it, his lip was badly cut. "Your stuff will be outside waiting for you when you get back to my house!" was my order. I got home very quickly and started packing his stuff. I threw it out of the door. Steve came home a little while later. He said "let me explain." I told him to get lost I wasn't interested. I told him to go away and if I ever saw him again I would call the Police. Mother came down and wanted to know what was going on. I told her what happened. Mother said everybody can make mistakes and tried to smooth things over. She said that Steve had nowhere to go and perhaps he should stay the night and maybe look for something tomorrow, and if he didn't find anything he could stay until he did find something. I told her that if Steve came back in the house I would go straight down to the nearest phone box and call the police and tell them everything. Mother knew I was in a strong position and that I would not back down. Steve just picked up his stuff and walked off. I didn't see him much after that, I know he was avoiding me as when I did see him he would walk the other way.

Chapter 53

That summer I went to Fecamp in France with Barry and Vale Harriers. It wasn't just athletics that was involved, it was football, and a few other sports. It was almost like a mini Olympics. It was great to be away from home. We stayed in a school hall, us boys in one hall, the girls in another. We were made to feel welcome, comfortable bed and clean linen hot showers when needed and decent food. Although I had to pick and choose some of the food as I was a little weary of trying anything too continental.

We had a few days training before the athletics competition started. Andrew Ireland taught us a technique called total relaxation. What a technique, I felt so calm and rested afterwards. We had time to go shopping and we were allowed a pretty free reign as to what we did when we were not training. I went to a couple of sports shops. I wanted a rugby ball. The ball that they were using in the five Nations Rugby Championship was a French ball with Lions branding on it. I thought as it was £15 in Wales it would be cheaper in France. How wrong could I be? The ball was three hundred and ninety five French Francs which at the time the exchange rate was about ten Francs to the pound worked out at just under twice the price back home.

I was asked to go out with the football team, the night before the athletics started. There was a little bit of trouble, but as soon as it started I made my way back to the digs. I didn't want to get involved in any trouble abroad. I turned out that some local men didn't like the football players, who were just having a quiet drink.

I did really well in my events; I came second in the hammer, and won the 1500 metres. I was a member of the 4x4oo metres team that won that event too. I mixed with competitors from the other countries. I got particularly well with a girl called Virgine. She was a middle distance runner from Fecamp so we had something in common. Virgine was also a rugby fan so we had lots to talk about although it was sometimes difficult as my French was nonexistent and Virgine's English was limited. We muddled through.

The last night that we were in Fecamp there was a meal and a disco. I spent most of the time with Virgine. After a slow dance together, she grabbed my hand and dragged me outside. She kissed me. I kissed her back. After what seemed like ages kissing outside, Virgine said we should go to her house. It was late and we had a curfew of eleven o'clock. I was a little naive I guess I couldn't understand why she was being so insistent that I go back to her house. We talked for an hour about all sorts of stuff. It got to 10.45 PM and that was just enough time to get back to the digs on foot as I had missed the bus. Virgine was still trying to persuade me to go back to her house, but I was adamant that I go back to meet curfew. Virgine gave me her address and phone number and told me to write.

The following morning it was time to leave. We had a leaving breakfast. We then started to load on to our buses. I loaded my bags and was just about to get on the bus when Virgine came running over. She flung her arms around me. She kissed me. All the athletics team came to my side of the bus and were looking out the window jeering. Virgine had tears in her eyes as she walked away. I had most of the team making fun of me all the way back home.

Chapter 54

The final year at school was quite different. Gibson and his crew continued to leave me alone, although there was always some snide comments and perhaps they would talk about me behind my back. The autumn term was quite busy at school, there was a definite change in the tempo and pressure. In January we were having our mock exams so that was the focus for the teachers. My focus was rugby. I was a regular in the school second XV. I wanted to play in the first team, however being fifth formers (Year eleven now) we were quite low in the pecking order as we had a sixth form and they made up the majority of the first XV. I did make a few appearances in the first team but not regularly which infuriated me. I put in so much hard work, and come training for the first and second XVs I made sure I outperformed the guys in my position. It didn't matter what I did I could not nail down a regular starting position. I blamed Huw Williams as he was in charge of the two teams. He never told me why he chose other boys instead of me and he never told me what I had to do to get a regular starting place, no matter how many times I asked. We did have a few fifth form games against other fifth form teams.

Chapter 55

A couple of weeks before Christmas the car broke down again. The engine ran and revved but there was hell of a noise and there was no drive to the wheels right in the middle of Cowbridge high street. I was ordered to push the car. Father stayed in the driver's seat so he could steer. Mother had no intention of helping at all. All she did was scowl and shout at me or father. Not exactly the best preparation for a rugby match, pushing a heavy estate car by myself with two occupants. I had warned father about buying this car, a Mark III Ford Cortina Estate 2.0L in beige with dark tan vinyl roof. Father said he needed the extra power. It was a heap of junk though, vastly over priced shed. Father was so determined to have this car, nothing would stop him. The salesman knew it too and didn't have to work hard to get the sale. He delivered the car and took away the blue Mark III Cortina saloon, that was newer and had less mileage. It was only a 1300cc and father wanted a 2000cc engine. That evening we went off to the workshop. As there was no drive I thought it was clutch or gearbox. Either way the gearbox had to come out. The car was on the ramp so access was not a problem. It took me an hour and a half to get the gearbox off. As the gearbox came away from the engine the flywheel came with it. The bolts holding the flywheel on had sheared. There was not a lot that could be done that night so, I put the gearbox in the boot and I pushed as my father steered, we put the car in the workshop car park.

The following day I looked at the workshop manual for the car. When I got home from school I went to the workshop and talked to a couple of the mechanics. They said the best thing would be to take the engine out and put a new crankshaft in. They told me that the bolts could be removed with a tap and dye set but there would probably be some damage to the crankshaft, and that it would most lightly be not straight and out of balance. My father had other ideas. He told me he was not paying for a new crankshaft, he would remove the bolts and re attach the fly wheel. Father got what he thought were the right bolts for the crankshaft. So that night I pushed the car onto the ramp as father steered. He set about drilling a hole in the sheared crankshaft bolts and inserting the extraction tools. The bolts eventually came out, but the thread in the crankshaft was shredded. So father set about cutting new thread , this made the bolt holes bigger and altered the balancing on the crankshaft even more. So once father had finished I had to install the clutch gearbox and prop shaft. When it was all back together the car started first time. It was working but the engine was not running right.

The car was parked up at home and did nothing much for the next couple of days. That weekend my father went to take mother to Rhoose to drop her off for her Friday night out with her friend Pauline. The car got half a mile when it broke down again. The same problem the bolts holding the flywheel to the crankshaft sheared. Mother went nuts. She insisted my father call her a taxi and pay for it, as she was not missing her night out.

It took my father a couple of weeks to track down a Ford Cortina Mk III Estate in beige with a brown vinyl roof that was the same as our car. He was going to use this as a donor car. The car he brought was driven to the workshop. It was a MoT failure and was sold for spares or repair. It was in worse condition than our car, which was hard. So my father's idea was to strip down the engine, take the crankshaft from the donor car, whose engine and gearbox were the only good things about it, and replace the crankshaft complete with flywheel in our car. So this work was started a couple of days before Christmas. It was stop and start work, especially stripping the crankshaft from the donor car. This car was outside and was a non runner as the carburettor had been removed to put on our car as it was better than the existing one on there. After several attempts, my father decided to get a fork lift and tip the car on its left hand side. His reasoning was that the crankshaft was at the bottom of the engine so it would be easier to get to that way. What my father failed to realise was that there was a cross member in the way so the engine sump could be unbolted but not moved out of the way to get at the crankshaft. What my father had failed to do was drain the engine oil so when the sump was unbolted and the seal broken oil went everywhere. So after what seemed like hours and several hammerings cutting bashing and some shouting my father got the sump out of the way. Then my father set about removing the crankshaft.

So Christmas Eve was spent stripping down the car to receive the donor crankshaft. My father had to disappear every now and then. He had to go pick up and drop off staff for the Aubrey Arms. By 10 PM I'd had enough. I locked the workshop up and went home shattered. My father got home about 1AM with mother. They came and woke me up. "So is it sorted?" was mother's rant. "No" was my reply. I explained what I had done and that I was too tired to carry on as I had been up since 5.00 AM. Mother went off on one, told me I had ruined Christmas, and how the hell were we going to get to her mother's on Christmas evening and her sisters on Boxing Day.

Christmas was the usual non event for me. A couple of weeks prior to Christmas mother asked me what I wanted. She told me to write down a list, I put down several things including some music albums. I was amazed to get 4 albums. Later Christmas day mother demanded the money. £20 was what she demanded. I was flabbergasted. She said she brought them as she thought I wanted them to give other people. What a crock. So I had a Christmas present from my parents, it was what I wanted; I know I paid for them.

So mid morning on Christmas day it was off to the workshop to try and put the car back together. It was a nightmare. Mother came up at 2.00 PM and told us our Christmas lunch was cold. She said she didn't bother keeping it warm as she couldn't care less. She said she had gone down the phone box and phoned her sister and told her that I hadn't finished fixing the car and that it was all my fault that we wouldn't make it to her mother's that afternoon. At about 4 PM there was a horn sounded outside the workshop. When I went outside it was my mother's sister Angela, she had come to pick us up and take us to her mother's house. So after cleaning up and a strip wash and getting changed it was off to her mother's for the usual Christmas evening family get together. It was the usual affair, shoes off at the door, brand new slippers that she had brought us for our Christmas present just for this day and best behaviour. It was a cold meat and salad buffet. As soon as I could I tucked in as I was really hungry as I had not eaten all day. Mother's mother criticised me for how much I ate. I wouldn't have minded but Simon and my father both had far more than me and both had eaten breakfast and lunch.

When Angela dropped us off that evening she said she would pick us up between 1 and 2 PM and she gave strict instructions not to work on the car as she didn't want to go to a dirty workshop to pick us up again. So Boxing Day we were picked up and went to Angela's. I spent most of the time in the play room. There were board games card games and puzzles. It was better than being with my parents.

Over the next couple of days, father decided he couldn't cope with doing the car, so he got a neighbour and a Forestry Commission mechanic to finish the work. I went up to see if I could help. Bob was a decent bloke who was ex REME and he knew his stuff. I explained what had been done and what I thought should have been done. I said as the donor engine was good before father took the carburettor off, it would have been easier to swap complete engines. Bob agreed, I just fetched and carried, but didn't do much as Bob was good and quick and didn't see me as a someone to do all the hard work. Bob realised that I wanted to learn and told me what he was doing and why. He got the car running but said he did hold out much hope for the car.

Chapter 56

In the New Year we played one game against a college from Neath. The guys from Neath were all nineteen and twenty, and the oldest boy in our team was sixteen. It was quite a chilly morning but nowhere near bad enough to call off the game, besides once into the game if you were running round enough you'd soon keep warm. The ground was not frozen so it was ok to play on. It was a very physical game one of the most physical games I have ever played in. Everybody in both teams gave 100%. I came off the pitch totally shattered and bruised all over. I also had a broken arm which I didn't realise at the time. We lost the game twenty points to nil. The score line didn't really reflect the game, it was far closer than that in performance. They were just so good at taking their chances. On the way back to the changing rooms, the opposition coach came up to me and praised me for my performance. It took me ages to shower and change, I was shattered battered and bruised in pain, but I felt really good about how I played. I was handed an envelope as I left the changing rooms, it was a book token for a man of the match performance. It was the first time I had received anything like that. I was really pleased. I had no intention of using it I was going to keep it with all my other medals and plaques.

The mock exams started and I was in so much pain with my right arm. I managed to do the exams. As the exams were mock exams they were administered by the school and were over and done within two weeks, the proper exams would take a lot longer, and some of the exams were only a couple of weeks away. I didn't do well in my mock exams. To be honest I was not prepared I didn't bother revising, my arm didn't help but it would not have had any bearing on my mock results. After the mocks finished I went to see my GP. He was obviously concerned and sent me for an x-ray. I went on the bus by myself. I knew I would only get grief if I went home and tried to get my father to take me. So I went to A&E first with the x-ray form. I had the x-ray and went back to A&E. The doctor told me I had an undisplaced fracture of my right forearm. I was put in a splint, one of those beige ones with Velcro and a metal strip. I was told that I had to wear it for four to six weeks. This didn't go down to well with school. I would still be in the splint when the early exams took place. That meant I had to go back to my GP and get a letter from him stating that I had a broken right arm and as I was right handed I would need some assistance with my exams. For the exams I was sat in a corner of the dining hall which was being used for exams apart from lunch time of course. I did the exams with my left hand and had more time to complete the exams.

There wasn't much rugby to be played in this part of the year. I guess it was down to the exams. I didn't miss much rugby while I was injured. I was more concerned about this than my studies. I did however continue competing in cross country. I was still competitive, finishing third with my arm in a splint.

Chapter 57

That spring as every spring was the Cowbridge Angling Club Annual Diner, which meant my father getting very drunk and coming home not long before I got up. So I had to walk and feed the horses as I generally did every year the morning after as he was in no fit state to drive. I got them done early as I then had to walk to the Aubrey Arms to clean Mr Bunn's Jaguar and get home in time to get the bus to Cowbridge for a rugby match. So I get home from cleaning the car and my father is in the front room, He was complaining of chest pain and numbness down his left arm. He described the pain as a crushing chest pain. Mother said "Don't listen to him, he's still pissed from last night. He should know better, serves him right he fucking well wouldn't take me! If he did he would have had to have driven so he wouldn't have drunk too much."

I had paid attention in First Aid at Air Cadets so I suspected he was having heart attack symptoms. However, my father was a bit of a faker, but this time I just knew he was not putting it on. So I spent the next thirty minutes trying neighbours to see if I could borrow a phone to call an ambulance. In the end the only person I could find was Mr Baker. He had a Rover 3.5 litre V8 in brown. He didn't have a phone but he said he was going to Cowbridge so he could drop us off at the doctors. Mr Baker drove his fast powerful car like a slug. On the A48 which is a sixty MPH limit he did not go over thirty MPH. So we eventually got to the doctors, father was put outside the doctor's office waiting his turn. Father didn't want me to leave. He knew the receptionist and when she passed he explained his symptoms to her. It was almost like he was looking for sympathy. My father went into the doctor's office by himself but was not in there long. The doctor came out and explained that my father was having a heart attack and that he would be going to hospital. The ambulance arrived in ten minutes. Father was collected from the surgery and put in a chair and wrapped in a blanket. I followed him out to the ambulance. Once in the ambulance father told me to go and play my game of rugby. We had a home match, so I would be home in a while. I went to the school and explained to Mr Randall what had happened. He advised me to play as it would take my mind off things but would understand if I didn't want to. I suppose I felt pressured to play, Mr Randall said as my father wanted me to play then I should play. So I did play, not one of my best games, not my worst either. I was also tired after all the running around I had done, but I also had father's illness on my mind. As soon as I was showered and changed I went home. Mother had gone to work, not much stopped her. When she got home I told her what had happened. "Some nurse you were!" was my scornful remark. On the Monday we were contacted by a woman called Shirley. She had sorted out some pension stuff for father and was from the company that the Forestry Commission was moving all its pensions and life insurance to. She had heard about father and offered us a lift into hospital that night. So she took mother myself and Caroline into the hospital. When we got there the doctor came over and explained what had happened and that father had had 3 heart attacks and that he would have to change his life style eat healthy give up smoking and take up exercise. Something that father would not take to and was very resistant too. The doctor also said that if it wasn't for me getting father help he would have died within an hour. I looked at mother, I felt justified. Even after the doctor explained everything she thought father was putting it on. A super nurse mother she was not. I didn't go and see father again in hospital. I did not feel comfortable going to hospital in Shirley's car. She went every night until he came home. I thought that was rather weird.

When father came out of hospital he was given strict instructions to lose weight cut down on drink and give up smoking. He was also told to take exercise. Father went out for a walk several times a day. His excuse was he was taking the exercise he was told to do. He was going out and smoking. He came back sucking on mints but smelling strongly of cigarettes. Mother ranted and raved that she knew he was sneaking out for a fag and that she hoped he killed himself smoking, then again she would have a cigarette in her mouth while saying this. She never cut down and continued to smoke forty a day.

Chapter 58

One of my last games for the school was against a touring side from the south coast of England. Unusually we were playing as a fifth form side (year eleven) instead of a first or second XV. I had my lower legs strapped up as since I had recovered from my broken arm, I had been training more and picked up some shin splints. It was more for protection. I normally rolled my socks down and my sleeves up, this was the only time since I first played flanker in the first year I had my socks pulled up. The game was a good physical contest. However, my opposite number was a really dirty player and had noticed the strapping on my legs and every ruck or maul would stamp or rake my lower legs. This went on all through the first half and to mid way through the second half. At this point I had taken the ball into a ruck and was at the bottom, I had a right stamping. I just laid there on my back, full of rage, I hated dirty play, if you gave your all and lost then that was great but if you had to cheat, that was just wrong.

The ball had moved to the other side of the field and the ref had blown up for a knock on by one of our players which meant a scrum to the opposition.

I lay on the ground, people sounded concerned, "Clive you alright?" "Clive you Alright?" At the third time of asking, people started coming over and they guy with the sponge bucket started to come over. I sat up "They've had it now!" I rolled my socks down and ripped off the strapping. I threw the strapping at someone on the sidelines and ran over to where the scrum was waiting for me. On the put in the other side won the ball, the passed it immediately to my opposite number. Bam I hit him like a steam train. The hardest tackle I had made at that point in my life. The tackle was totally legal but so hard. I kept hold of him and drove him onto the ground. I knew he was hurt, but I didn't escape unhurt. I dislocated my right shoulder, but I was so full of adrenalin I didn't feel it. Two people had to carry my opposite number off. I felt justified. I was on fire, I made several telling breaks and scored 2 tries and was involved in the other two that we scored after their open side flanker went off. They sort of crumpled after he went off.

After the game we were all walking back to the changing rooms. Their injured boy was left on the side of the pitch, still obviously in a lot of pain and a little out of it. The opposition coach had to be reminded that their injured boy was still there and still hurt and perhaps he should be seeking medical help. The coach said he didn't have time as they were leaving to go back home as soon as everybody was changed. He was quickly told that he would seek medical help for his injured players before going home. They had to use both of their subs so both needed looking at by a doctor. The local beat Bobby walked over and said he would ensure that the two boys would be seeing a doctor.

After I showered, while getting dressed I had real problems moving my right shoulder. It was very painful. I managed to get dressed. My father was actually waiting for me after the game. Something he had never done before. I had mentioned to one of our PE staff about my shoulder. He said it looked like it was dislocated. He told my father that I needed to go to hospital to have my shoulder looked at. My father was not happy. It meant that he would have to drop the food for my siblings off at the stables, and then take me to the hospital. I was in the hospital for just over an hour, and that included x-rays. It was confirmed my shoulder was dislocated It was manipulated back into place quite easily and I was put in a sling given exercises and pain killers. My father was not happy, it meant that he would have to feed and see to the horses by himself for the next couple of weeks. I only had a week at school before end of spring term and managed to stay away from certain people.

A couple of weeks later Bluey the smaller pony died. It looked like he got stuck in mud and collapsed and died. Father had moved the horses to this particular field as it was so cheap. It was so cheap as it was a muddy bog and hadn't been used for years, as it wasn't fit for anything. Looking back putting the horses in there was such a bad idea and made no sense it wasn't fit for anything. Father decided to move the remaining horse Duke to the stables. His thinking was that he might be able to earn a little bit of money if they could use him on their rides.

Simon finished school early and did not sit any exams, he went to work at the stables, on a Youth Training Scheme (YTS). Mother and Father were telling people that Simon was being trained to manage the place one day. It was hinted that with Simon working at the stables and making Duke available for rides, was the reason that they were not paying livery. While Simon was working at the stables mother and father tried to do everything they could to involve themselves in the hunting set. Attending every hunt, making food, especially for the boxing day hunt. Mother made a huge amount of mince pies for the boxing day hunt. She was handing them round like they were going out of fashion. Insisting on people taking a mince pie. I was enlisted to carry the pies. Father did what he did best talk and talk and talk, all of it a load of rubbish. It was quite funny seeing all the well to do hunt members take a mince pie, take a bite, the faces that were pulled was funny. Obviously they didn't go down well, people were "Accidently" dropping them or putting them in their pockets. I started seeing warnings about the mince pies. Shaken heads warning not to take one. There was loads left. "Oh well more for me" was father's claim, as he tucked in to two at a time.

It wasn't long till Simon's YTS finished. Needless to say he was not taken on permanently. He took a job as a farm labourer.

Chapter 59

I had been to training at Barry and Vale Harriers all winter even through my injuries. I worked around them. By the time the summer term came I was at my fittest and faster than ever on the track and the improvements were big. So much so that Bridger was waiting to see what events I was doing before committing to what event he was doing. At the start of the term was the Welsh Schools competition at my club. Mr Huw Williams decided not to take me, so I went as a guest and ran for my club not the school. Bridger didn't know it but I was running the 1500 metre steeplechase. I had quite a job getting to the track, three busses and a two mile jog with my running kit to make it on time. I warmed up thoroughly and felt really good. When the gun went off I immediately went into the lead. My thoughts were I was going to push as fast as I could. I was really confident I was pushing as hard as I could. If I was going to lose then whoever beat me would have to run bloody fast. I started to stretch out 600 metres from home really stretching out the guys behind me. With 400 metres to go I was expecting to accelerate again, but I didn't have the energy my legs were starting to feel like lead. Bridger and my club team mate Colin Higgnel past me, I was struggling to stay with them. Andrew Ireland was shouting at me trying to encourage me, he was willing me on, the support lifted me, but I still couldn't find any more speed. With 300 metres to go I was passed by another runner, I was down to fourth. I was able to hang on to the guy in third place, my hurdling was still good but struggled at the water jump. Into the final bend I was running as fast as I could, at the final hurdle I made up ground on third place he was tiring but I just didn't have enough to pass him. In the end I was less than ten seconds behind first place. I had taken fifteen seconds off my personal best though, but I was disappointed, I thought I could win. I beat my school's other runner by forty seconds so I felt justified. Bridger knew his days as the best in the school were numbered. I knew I had more to come and so did Andrew Ireland. It was the last time I would lose to Bridger in fair competition.

At school I had acquired an ally, Philip Marsh. He was aggrieved at the unfairness the Huw Williams dished out and the favouritism that Bridger got. Philip was a decent guy and he saw the funny side of Bridger's club initials. Cardiff Amateur Athletic Club, CAAC and he used to call it caac as in slang for poo. Philip was a decent runner and he really supported my Athletic club.

When my main exams were upon me I decided that I should actually do some work and start revising. I did some revision but not as much as I should have done. I felt I did ok in my exams. I struggled with the Welsh talking exam that was the only exam that I found difficult. I found the Maths exam easiest of all. It would be several weeks before I found out my results and I wasn't going to waste time worrying about it. My last day at school was June twenty third apart from school sports day.

A few days after my last exam I bumped into a girl from my year. We got on at school. We exchanged the usual pleasantries. She asked what I was up to over the next few days. I told her that I was going swimming in Cardiff at the Empire pool tomorrow. She said that sounds good and she asked what bus I was catching. We arranged to meet on the bus along with a couple of others. We had a great time at the pool, just messing around. I had a bit of a swim to get some exercise and ease some stiffness. When I finished the girl came over and splashed me, and I splashed her back, then all of a sudden her bikini top fell down exposing her right breast. She looked a little embarrassed but she was not that quick to cover back up. It was the first time I had seen a naked breast, my eyes nearly popped out of my head.

We left shortly after. I felt a little sheepish I guess she did as well. We sort of slipped away by ourselves. as we got near the bus station she slipped her hand in mine. I couldn't believe that a girl from my school would be interested in me.

We didn't say much on the bus. We pasted my stop and I stayed on until her stop. We got off and started to walk to her house. She pulled me to the side of the lane and into a gate way. She kissed me and I responded. After a few minutes she pulled away. She told me she had a boyfriend, and it wasn't fair to him. She told me that if it wasn't for her boyfriend she would love to go out with me, but she felt guilty. I knew it was too good to be true. I was a little taken aback but not really surprised. Good things like that didn't happen to me. She told me that she really liked me and kissed me before running off home. I was a little confused. I decided to walk the mile or so home, it was a nice afternoon and I needed to clear my head.

I was brought back down with a thump when I got home. "Where the fuck have you been?" was mother's demand. "I told you I was going in to Cardiff today." I said. "Well you should have been here hours ago to sort out tea so I could go to work. You've made me late for work, and all they've had is a sandwich!" There was no point in arguing I just walked off and left her to it. I went to my room and laid on my bed. I put a tape on and my headphones and thought about what happened today. When the tape finished I switched over to the radio. I was trying to go through the day and make sense of it. Perhaps there was no sense to be made. I would have to put it out of my mind as it wasn't going to happen again was it?

On sorts day I was really up for the race. I knew I would beat Bridger and in front of the whole school that would be so good. So when we lined up for the race there was our year and the 6th Form in one race. So I made my way to the outer lanes, I wanted a clean get away. One of the 6th formers lined up inside me right on my left shoulder. That didn't bother me as I knew I was a lot faster than him. The gun went off, I felt pain in my right foot and I limped to the edge of the track. There was blood everywhere, I had been spiked, my running spikes were torn apart and there was two wounds three centimetres long to the edge of my foot and right through my foot. Glan Williams shouted at me, "Go and beat him Clive!" I set off like a demented whirling dervish, there was pain and blood but at the moment that didn't matter. I was 300 metres behind but I wanted to catch up and I was fuming. I made up most of the ground but it was too much to make up. I finished third. I crossed the line and was storming up to the guy who spiked me. He was wearing 18 mm Javelin spikes. I was shouting at him, I was going to smash his face in. Bridger was laughing "How's your foot Thomas?" Bridger was going to get it second. I was going to flatten them both. My first punch connected flush on the chin of the guy who spiked me. Glan Williams grabbed me "Come on Clive lets go" was his instruction. He took me to lower playing field. My running spikes were ruined. My foot was a mess there were two wounds that went from the side of my foot to the edge and right through. Glan got the school nurse over and they patched me up. Stitches were going to be difficult unless I was on crutches so the wounds were held together by steri strips bandage and tape. Luckily that part of the foot is not that thick. Glan was pretty mad and said he was going to try and get some people disqualified. It was obvious that a few people were in on it. I had no intention of going back to that school, and the school didn't matter to me. I had more important races to run than a poxy school sports day, I had been deliberately injured just to stop me beating Bridger. He didn't beat me by fair means, next time I raced him he would lose I was sure of that.

I was competing that Sunday so needed new spikes. I was running the 1500m so needed to have some decent running spikes. I had to make my way in to Cardiff to Bernie Plain's sports shop. Bernie was an accomplished runner and gave discounts to young athletes from local clubs. As I was buying the spikes I went with Bernie's recommendation a pair of Nikes, they were so much better than my old Adidas spikes, and I looked forward to competing in them even with two gouges out of my left foot.

I did ok in the race but nowhere near my best. My foot was really sore and hindered my race, and perhaps competing in the week might not have been the best idea as fatigue may have been a factor. I did my best and Andrew knew that and that was all he ever asked, and rewarded effort with praise help and advice. If you put in the effort regardless of the result Andrew put in the effort with you and spent time coaching and giving nutritional advice.

Chapter 60

At the end of summer term was the annual twin town exchange come games. My age team mates and I were not competing but we were asked to come down and help with the athletics competition. We had a few days training and qualified as Amateur Athletics Association (AAA) track and field judges. We helped with the officiating of the track and field. It was quite a summer festival, and I quite enjoyed the time I spent there. We also trained while at the track before the competition began. The weather was fabulous for the week of the games.

Jo told me Suzi was staying at her house and although there were events planned she wanted to see me. We spent the afternoon together talking we went for a walk. As we walked Suzi slipped her hand in mine and held my hand tightly as if she didn't want to let go. When we got back to Jo's house and Jo said she had to go into town to buy something for her mother, which left Suzi and I alone. We talked for a while, Put on some music. but we kept on looking at each other, I moved closer and I was very nervous. I held her hand, Suzi snuggled into me. I kissed her for what seemed like ages. We talked for ages until Jo came home. I told Suzi that I was going to join the Army and in all likelihood I would be posted to Germany. Suzi said she would be happy for me to be posted to Germany as it would be easier for us to see each other. We spent a lovely day together, parting we said we would write and I said I would let her know where I got posted too once I finished my training. This was however the last time we would meet. We wrote for a few years but we never actually met again.

Chapter 61

By the time I was sixteen I was running in the 4x400 relay, 1500 metres steeplechase and throwing the hammer for my club. Odd combination it might have been, but I loved it. I must admit I was happy to please my coaches as whatever my results they knew I always gave 100% and I was given the praise that was so lacking at home. I did get to represent the British Young Athletes League not long before my 16th birthday in a competition against Australia and some local clubs. The event was held at Cwmbran. Unlike most athletics tracks in Wales, Cwmbran had a modern up to date track with a synthetic surface. Most other clubs had old fashioned cinder tracks. Some clubs still had grass tracks. I did run injured in the steeple chase but did come in the top three. When I was fourteen my sister decided that she wanted to join the athletics club. When this happened my father decided to get involved and got onto the club committee. Mind you the only time he attended competitions was when my sister was competing at our home track. My neighbour Stuart Husband also joined the club, and his mother or father usually took us to or collected us from training. Mr Andrew Ireland was the club coach, he spent a lot of time with me. I guess he saw some potential in me, but I suppose he was a little frustrated at times as my time was split between rugby and athletics. The summer of my 16th birthday I got really focussed on my athletics, training every day to the schedule that Andrew had set me. I was also training with Colin Hignall quite a bit, but when I was making big improvements I started to train more with Paul Williams, who was the World under sixteen 800 metre champion. Although not in Paul's league at 800 metres training with him lifted my performances in the 1500 metres and 1500 metres steeplechase. My 800 metres time also tumbled. My personal best being one minute fifty two seconds. This was some five seconds slower than Pauls though.

I had to go into school to collect my O level and CSE results. Everyone seemed to arrive at the same time. I guess people were eager to get their results. I got there early as I wanted to go into Barry for some training at Jenner Park and had arranged to meet up with Andrew Ireland for some coaching.

Gibson and his crew made some remarks about me turning up to get my failure sheets. This was like water off a ducks back to me. It wasn't said to my face but loud enough for me to hear. I notice they didn't have the courage to say it to my face. So I got my two print outs one for O levels and one for CSEs. Two C grades at O level and four Grade 1s at CSE. CSE Grade ones were treated as a C Grade or higher at O level. A couple of the girls in my year were genuinely pleased for me. I did better than I thought I would and better than most people predicted. A couple of girls took great delight in telling Gibson and his gang how well I'd done especially as some of them hadn't done as well as they should have or expected to do. I wasn't really bothered I knew what I was going to do, and these small minded petty little boys will always be petty small minded little boys, who revel in and believe their own egos.

I met a guy called Justin at my Gran's house. He was a friend of my cousins. He was an interesting bloke. I learned he was twenty four and owned his own house and had a good job. I stayed with him a couple of times, he was very open and honest and generous. I learned some guys had taken advantage of him and his generosity. I encouraged him to go to the police as he had been stolen from abused and blackmailed. I guess in some ways we had a little in common. Justin tried to give me his spare bicycle but I didn't think that was right. I told him, if I could afford it I would buy it off him. I didn't have the money by the time I joined the Army. Maybe that was for the best as Simon would have got hold of it with father's help and wrecked it.

That summer I went to Sutton Coalfield the Army Selection Centre in the Midlands. There we had physical tests in the gym and written tests. We also had a few interviews with different officers trying to assess us. I could have done with going to Sutton Coalfield either 2 weeks earlier or a few weeks later. I had a broken big toe that happened during pre season training for Cowbridge Rugby club. It didn't stop me running but it did hamper me. The final physical test was a one mile run. The PTIs had been talking to me as I was one of very few who turned up with decent running kit. My times for the season were far quicker than the course record for potential Junior Leaders in the Army. The run went quite well and I led until about half way. Then a guy who ended up in the same troop as I passed me. I recognised him from the athletic circuit but did not know his name at this stage. He was from another Welsh club and I had never lost to him, but on this day I was struggling. I suppose a combination of a broken toe, not training for a couple of weeks and doing more rugby training than athletics training meant that I was not at my best. I was the type of person who had to train hard to get results and not as naturally talented at running as most of the people I had competed against. I did come a close second but was still disappointed with my time and performance. Once showered and changed we had a final interview with an officer. We talked about various regiments and corps. When I said that I could be interested in the Royal Regiment of Wales the officer told me that if I was to put down that my choices as an infantry regiment he would reject my application and that I should think about one of the corps and a trade. We talked about the pros and cons of several corps and in the end we agreed that my first choice was the Junior Leaders Regiment Royal Corps of Transport, second was Junior Leaders Regiment Army Air Corps and third choice was Junior Leaders Regiment Royal Engineers. I was asked to leave the room for a little while as the officer wanted to discus my application. Fifteen minutes later I was called back in. my second and third choices were fully subscribed for the next two intakes. There was a possibility that I could make the September intake but it that was unlikely, but they would like to offer me a place in the January 1984 intake of the Junior Leaders Regiment Royal Corps of Transport. I was really pleased.

On the train home there were a couple of us who had been to the Army selection Centre. It was a little load but we weren't bothering anyone, we were just having a laugh. A couple of girls passed us, and I was egged on to try chatting them up. Another lad joined me was we talked to the girls. They were about our age, the one who I took an interest in me was a girl called Kirsty and she was from Lydney near Gloucester. It wasn't long before the train arrived at Kirsty's stop. We exchanged addresses and we agreed to write.

When September came, my mother insisted that I go and sign on. I was waiting to join the Army and had to wait until January to start. In those days I had to travel to Llantwit Major to sign on. As I lived so far away and it was awkward to get to, I was given a postal signing. I think I got £16.50 per week. My mother demanded £10 per week for my "Keep." I was expected to buy most of my own food. Simon was signing on as unemployed, but he was working on a local farm, cash in hand. I was not happy with this. When the farm where Simon worked, asked me to work cash in hand for the potato harvest, I jumped at the chance. It was decent money. I worked hard, but I did declare what I earned. My mother went mad, she said she was losing £10 a week from my dole so I would have to make that up out of my wages and pay the extra £10. Simon was getting £2 per hour and generally was at work for about 50 hours a week. The farmer was a shrewd man and paid Simon £80 per week and said that was more than fair for the amount of work Simon actually did. My mother was expecting me to be on the same money, and demanded £50 per week for my "keep." She also expected me to give her £10 on top of that for what she said was the money she lost due to me declaring my earnings. My first week I took home £120, I didn't tell my mother how much I earned, she would have expected more money from me. I spent 6 weeks on the potato harvest and generally brought home the same money each week. When the work stopped and I was back on the dole, my mother was not happy. She tried to argue that I would have to pay her £15 per week so it was not so much of a loss for her. I refused and only gave her £10. I stuck to my guns. I was still picking up pocket money cleaning a couple of cars a week. My mother was not aware that I was still doing this, if she was, she would be expecting a cut for that money as well. I'm all for paying my way, but when I was working for cash in hand, the money I was giving my mother was more than twice the weekly family food shopping bill.

I got a message from Mr Glan Williams, asking me to go and see him. I went a couple of days later. Glan knew of my plans to join the Army and asked when I was starting. When I replied January 1984, Glan asked me if I was busy Tuesday after school. I replied that I wasn't so Glan asked if I would come and help him with training the first and second year's rugby teams. I was only too happy. Glan made sure I was never out of pocket for helping coach the teams. I was also asked to help with coaching the mini rugby at Maendy County Primary School as Mr George had left. I was happy to help with this as well. However, Maendy was a very small school and was struggling to raise a team, it was decided that the school would only play a couple of games against other schools, and that most of the rugby that they played was in their P.E. lesson.

Chapter 62

I played for Cowbridge Rugby club on Saturdays. I reasoned that there was not much point in going for trials at one of the big clubs which I had been asked to go for as I was joining the Army. If I was good enough then I could pursue my rugby through the Army I thought. I was not intimidated by any of the guys. I found it quite a challenge being so young, playing against full grown men. I had a distant cousin playing for Cowbridge, Trevor Morgan. We were very competitive. Whenever Trevor got the ball in training, I would shout "He's MINE!" and tackle Trevor as hard as I could. We had so much fun, Trevor would also return the favour when I had the ball. I was a lot faster than Trevor and was sometimes able to out run and slip away from Trevor. Sometimes however, Trevor used his superior knowledge and experience to catch me. I would take the hard thump of a tackle from him and get up smiling. I loved it. I put the same energy into playing rugby at senior age grade rugby as I did as when I was at school. I showed no fear on the pitch. However, as I was young and small at 5'8" and about eleven and a half stones I was not really big enough to play my usual position. As I was fast and I could run with the ball I was moved to the wing. I did struggle a little in my first few games but it was not long before I felt comfortable in the position. In some ways I was ahead of my time as I was a small winger who could and would tackle anybody on the pitch. The only time I had any real trouble tackling a guy was a second row from another local club who was 6'10" and about twenty eight stones. I guess he could have played anywhere in the pack, come to think of it he could have been the whole pack. I did tackle him and eventually he did go to ground I wrapped my arms round his thighs as best as I could and slide down grabbing tighter and tighter until my arms were around his ankles and over he went. I did have a little help with some of my side's pack piling on to assist him going over. Surprisingly the giant didn't last long, he was not very resilient couldn't take much punishment and had no stamina. After the first twenty minutes he went off and that was the last I saw of him.

As I was so young and small I had been started off in the thirds, although after my performance against the giant I was promoted to the seconds. My first game I scored a nice try. From our 22 the ball was kicked down field. I chased, it went deep into our opponents twenty two. Their full back scampered back and collected the ball, as I was bearing down the full back kicked the ball to try and clear his line, I was on top of him and charged the ball down, I kicked the ball over the try line and pounced on the ball, scoring our first try, and near the posts to make the conversion easier. What made the try memorable was, as I was getting up after scoring, I had just got to my feet when the opposition full back tackled me from behind and I had left the ball on the ground. The try was awarded, the conversion scored and as we were waiting for the ball to come back to half way, the ref ran to the halfway line and awarded a penalty against the full back and sent him off. It was a little used rule, a deliberate foul after the try was scored. I had not heard of the rule before and thinking about it later it is a good rule which should be used more often. I don't know if the rule is still applicable today.

Our rugby club was like a feeder club for some of the local bigger clubs. It was not unusual for one or more of the players to be called up into one of the bigger clubs in the higher divisions. This happened to me a few times. It was a bit strange going to another club for one training session and playing for them for one game and then back to my own club. I did have some approaches from a couple of clubs and two rugby league clubs, but rugby league was a dirty word in Wales at that time and something I would not even contemplate, even if they were offering a lot of money.

A couple of weeks before Christmas my left arm was swollen and sore. I carried on playing rugby but it was definitely a problem. I went to my GP who wrote a letter and told me to go to A & E which I did. It turned out that I had an infection in my lymph gland in my elbow that was probably caused by a scratch on my hand. The only conclusion that the doctors could come up with after doing several tests was that it was a cat that scratched me and caused the infection. I was put in a sling for a week and given powerful antibiotics. It did settle down with treatment.

While my Arm was in a sling I went to Kirsty's house in Lydney Gloucestershire. I had been invited down for her sister's party. I was away for a couple of days and had a great time. Kirsty's sister was a policewoman. It was nice to be with a real family who obviously cared about each other. The first night I stayed I went baby sitting with Kirsty. The second day was spent preparing for the party. I had a bath and got ready, my hair was still damp, I had given it a quick comb as usual. Kirsty and her sister said that I wasn't going to the party like that and set about gelling and blow drying my hair. It was the first party I had really enjoyed. I didn't feel guilty eating or having something to drink.

The following day it was time to leave. I was saddened to leave. I felt really comfortable in Lydney, and felt I could be myself and relax, going back home meant back to the usual rubbish.

December twenty third 1983 I had an appointment at the Army Careers Office to take my Oath of Allegiance. My mother decided to come with me to make sure that I didn't change my mind. I had no intention of changing my mind. I was joining the Army and there was little she could do to stop it. On the way in, mother said she wanted to get me a smart jacket or blazer. So after looking in a couple of shops I picked out a nice double breasted blazer. When it came time to pay, mother turned round and said "I hope you don't expect me to pay for that!" I thought typical, she wanted to get me a blazer and I pay for it.

In the old days they called taking the Oath of Allegiance taking the King's/Queens shilling. However on that day I got a £5 note. I decided not to tell mother she would probably want some of it. I was really proud when I took the Oath of Allegiance. I was in a room with a few other guys, some of whom I knew from other schools rugby teams. There was one guy in particular who was a bit loud and trying really hard to be a comedian called Chris. He knew me, but to be honest I still have no recollection of who he is and I don't recall ever playing against him, although there was another guy who I remember from rugby. The ceremony lasted all of five minutes. We were shown into a room we all raised one hand and read from a card. We were give the £5 signed for the money and that was it. We were given our travel instruction and rail warrants in an envelope and told we would be met at Bath Railway station on January 10th 1984 and told not to be late. In the envelope there was time slots and what trains we were expected to be on. I was due to get to Bath Railway Station between 10AM and 12PM or between 1000 Hrs and 1200 Hrs in Army time. The day my life would start for real.

My first match back after the infection was Christmas Eve. We had an away game, I was selected in the second team as I had missed a couple of games. The game was going pretty well until not long before the end of the first half. There was a ruck on our ten metre line and about ten metres in from the left touch line. The ball popped out of the ruck. I went for it I accelerated as fast as I could. As I ran I bent down and scooped the ball up. Just as I was straightening up I saw there was no one covering and a sure try was on. Then bang the opposition hooker dived out of the ruck to try and get the ball. His forehead connected with my mouth. The next thing I knew I was on the sidelines being held up by two club members. There was a lot of blood, I was all over the place and couldn't stand unaided. An ambulance had been called but they were called back and the ambulance cancelled. My teeth were smashed. I was taken by car along with the opposition hooker to hospital. I had one broken tooth one tooth that they saved but had been knocked against the roof of my mouth so the nerve was dead along with some chipped teeth and a broken nose and concussion. I had my nose straightened three hours emergency dentistry before being allowed home. They wanted to keep me in but as my mother said she was a nurse they let me go. The opposition hooker had seven stitches in his forehead and concussion. Not my best Christmas Eve, even by my standards.

Christmas Day was the usual let down. I got an electric razor form my parents. A real good electric razor a Braun. Thing was I paid for it. We did the usual thing at my mother's parents house.

Boxing day there was a knock on the door. It was a couple of the guys from the rugby club. They insisted that I go with them to watch the game I would have played in had I not been injured. We won the match and I was treated to some Christmas cheer. It was the first time I had been drunk. Most of the team wanted to buy me a drink. I was supposed to have been playing but for obvious reasons was unable to play and was feeling a bit sorry for myself until the guys from the club turned up. I eventually was allowed to leave after having way too much to drink. I have no idea how long it took me to get home, all I remember was taking a short cut home over Cowbridge Downs. There was a horrific murder of a taxi driver there about four or five years previous and I saw someone walking their dog. I was so drunk I was convinced they were the taxi driver murderer. Obviously totally daft and I staggered towards home after trying to slur some words at the innocent person 100 metres away.

Things were pretty quiet between Christmas and new year. I kept my head down and out of mother's way. I did go to my local dentist who did some more work on my busted teeth. I had some cement between both front teeth to give the one with the dead nerve a splint so the gum and bone could heal around the tooth. He also did a proper root canal.

Chapter 63

10th of January 1984. I had packed the previous night. I just had to wash shave and get dressed. I had a cup of tea and left the house. I walked up to the bus stop in plenty of time to catch the 9 o'clock bus. Just before the bus arrived, mother appeared puffing away. "What are you doing here?" I was surprised that she came. Perhaps she was coming to see me off. "I'm coming to the station to make sure you get on that train. I don't want you changing your mind." was her scornful remark.

I got on the bus paid for my single to Cardiff. I sat near the front of the bus. Mother walked straight passed me to the back of the bus. In those days you were allowed to smoke at the back of the bus. She sat down and lit another cigarette with the butt of her last cigarette.

The bus arrived at Cardiff bus station. Mother stayed in her seat at the back of the bus for the whole journey puffing away constantly on her cigarettes. It's just a short walk from the bus station to the railway station so I made my way across. Mother followed just behind. When I got to the station I presented my Army rail warrant and was given my ticket by the ticket officer. I went to walk to the platform and pass through the ticket control. Mother said "Well, aren't you going to get me a platform ticket?" it was a demand not a request. "No it's ok you can say goodbye now." "I want to make sure you get on that train." I walked off handing my ticket to the inspector and onto the platform. Mother appeared behind me. "The ticket inspector let me through."

The train arrived on time. I got on the train and opened the window. I thought I'd better say goodbye to mother. Before I could say anything she turned round and said "Just make sure you don't come back!"

I didn't say a word, just closed the window and went and took my seat. The journey to Bath required me to change trains at Bristol Parkway, but it seemed to fly by. When I arrived in Bath I was directed outside and onto a white Army bus. I was full of anticipation excitement even a little fear. I had no idea of how long the journey took but we arrived at Azimghur Barracks just outside the village of Colerne. The bus pulled up outside the cook house. There was a NAAFI and function room upstairs. There were 3 tables one for each squadron. On entering I was met by a soldier in No two best Dress with a clip board. He asked me for my letter. I was told I would be in 30 Squadron and told to make my way to their table. Between the soldier and the tables were a few soldiers in coloured tracksuits. I was approached by a couple of soldiers in blue tracksuits and asked if I played an instrument and if I would like to join the Regimental band. I said I didn't play anything and wasn't interested in the band. They explained that regardless of what Squadron I was assigned I could go to 57 Squadron if I wanted to join the band. Another couple of soldiers came over in red tracksuits and told me not to listen to the guys from 57 Squadron and the band was rubbish, there was a bit of light hearted banter. I went to the 30 Squadron desk. Two soldiers were dressed in No two Best Dress and gave me a card with my regimental number and the barracks address. I was told to wait with a couple of other guys and we would be shown to our accommodation block.

We were escorted to our block. We were shown to the top floor of a two story building. We were shown into a room, allocated a bed and given a red tracksuit with a big white R.C.T. cap badge on the left chest. We were told to put our tracksuits on and we would form up outside when told.

This was Gloucester Troop 30 (Junior Leaders) Squadron Royal Corps of Transport. The day my life began!

About The Author

After joining the Army in 1984 a serious knee injury threatened my career. After a series of operations I passed out and proceeded to Lecconfield for my trade training, after a short detachment in London I was Posted to Germany. After a couple of years I was posted to 5 Airborne Brigade in Aldershot. While serving here I met my wife Karen. Being married along with the birth of my son, my priorities changed and I left the Army with an Exemplary record in August 1991. After a couple of years going from job to job, injuries sustained in the Army forced a career change. After further education as a mature student and the birth of my daughters I embarked on a career in IT, working mainly within Government and MoD establishments.

Printed in Great Britain
by Amazon